MARRIAGE,

DIVORCE, & REMARRIAGE
FROM A BIBLICAL PERSPECTIVE

BY DR. JACK SCHAAP

CREDITS
Project Manager: David Jorgensen
Assistant: Rochelle Chalifoux
Transcription: Nan Bell
Cover Design: Douglas Wruck
Page Design and Layout: Linda Stubblefield
Proofreaders: Rena Fish, Linda Flesher, Karen Kalapp, Julie Richter, and Cindy Schaap

To order additional copies of this book, please contact:
PREPARE NOW RESOURCES®
507 State Street • Hammond, Indiana 46320
hylespublications.com
info@hylespublications.com

Dedication

I affectionately dedicate this book to my sweetheart, partner, confidante, best friend, lover, and wife. Thirty-four years ago I asked out a 17-year-old high school senior. From that very first date, we have been love-struck. We married two years later and promised each other that divorce would never be an option for

MARRIAGE, DIVORCE, & REMARRIAGE

us. We are more crazy in love with each other now than either of us could have imagined back then.

While we have witnessed and grieved the decay and eventual divorces in relationships among many of our friends, loved ones, and fellow companions of life, Cindy and I have only redoubled our commitment to each other with each marital failure we encounter. Our "secret" is this: marry well, work at it every day, and lean on God's grace.

My hope in writing this book is that those who may be contemplating divorce or those who may have been injured by divorce would find the grace of God to do the right thing and hopefully experience a relationship of marriage that is akin to the one Cindy and I enjoy.

– Pastor Jack Schaap

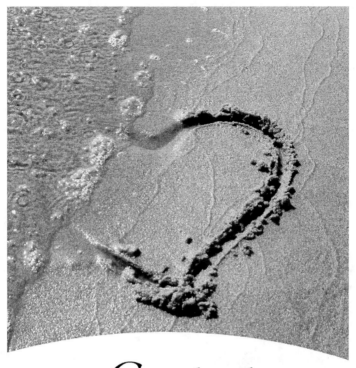

Contents

MARRIAGE, DIVORCE, & REMARRIAGE

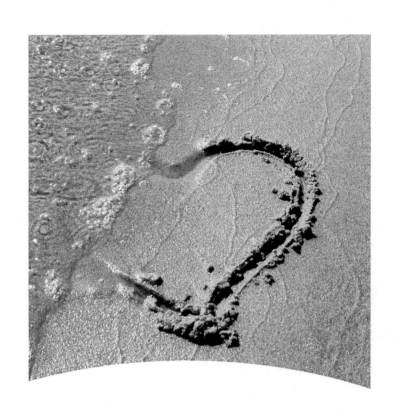

Introduction

QUESTIONS AND CONTROVERSY abound about the issue of marriage, divorce, and remarriage. The same questions arose not only in the days of Jesus but also in the days of Moses, nearly 1,500 years before the birth of Christ. These same controversies of Biblical days still surround marriage, divorce, and remarriage today, giving rise to questions such as the following:

- Who is allowed to divorce?
- Is divorce ever permissible?
- Does God always hate divorce?
- If someone is divorced, may the person re-marry?
- What are the allowable conditions for remar-riage?
- Is there such a thing as an exception clause in marriage that allows a Biblical divorce?

These kinds of questions have generated controversies that have been debated for the better part of 4,000 years. The question is, "Do the continued controversies address the core issues and the problems that arise with broken marriages?" Author Andrew J. Cherlin states, "No trend in the American family life since World War II has received more attention or caused more concern than the rising rate of divorce."[1] In their book entitled *Saving Your Second Marriage Before It Starts,* Dr. Les Parrott and his wife, Dr. Leslie Parrott, share some pertinent statistics about marriage, divorce, and remarriage and about modern society's almost casual attitude toward God's first institution—marriage.

In the 1930s, one out of seven marriages ended in divorce. In the 1960s, it was one out of four. Of the 2.4 million couples who will get married this year [2001] in the United States, it is predicted that at least 50 percent of the marriages will not survive. And most startling, of those getting married for a second time, 60 percent will not make it. For too many couples, marriage has become "till divorce do us part."[2]

Conflicts and disputes arise because everyone has a different background with a different upbringing.

INTRODUCTION

Most disagreements come down to what we have been taught, what we have read, or what we heard someone say that sounded acceptable. The only answer to controversy is to open the Bible to see exactly what the Scripture says. The more people tend to state their "feelings" as opposed to following Biblical facts, the more they tend to become like people in the book of Judges where every man did that which was right in his own eyes. That philosophy gives rise to everyone's having his own opinion regarding his personal perception of truth rather than drawing reasonable conclusions from what the Truth says. Christians must always keep and maintain a temperate disposition and avoid making a personally hostile attack on someone—no matter how vitriolic another's words may be or how demeaning and harsh their sentiment.

Christians must always stay with the Truth and bring people back to the Word of God. This book takes that position—searching out the truth about marriage, divorce, and remarriage from the Word of God—the Christian's final authority. The bottom line is that the Christian's final authority in all matters of faith and practice is indeed the Word of God—whether or not he chooses to agree with what the Bible says. This book will address what the Christian's Final Authority says about the matter of marriage, divorce, and remarriage.

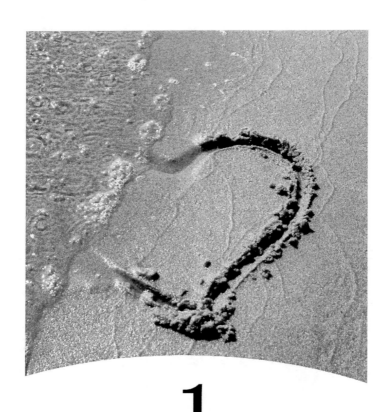

1

Marriage,
DIVORCE, & REMARRIAGE

Marriage is not a machine that needs routine maintenance to keep it functioning, but a supernatural event founded upon a mutual exchange of holy pledges. Above all, marriage is a deep, mysterious, and unfathomable endeavor.

– Parrott

"*The* Pharisees also came unto him, tempting him, and saying unto him, Is it lawful for a man to put away [divorce] his wife for every cause? ⁴And he answered and said unto them, Have ye not read, that he which made them **at the beginning** made them male and female, ⁵And said, For this cause shall a man leave father and mother, and shall cleave to his wife: and they twain shall be one flesh? ⁶Wherefore they are no more twain, but one flesh. What therefore God hath joined together, let not man put asunder. ⁷They say unto him, Why did Moses then command to give a writing of divorcement, and to put her away? ⁸He saith unto them, Moses because of the hardness of your hearts suffered you to put away your wives: but **from the beginning** it was not so. ⁹And I say unto you, Whosoever shall put away his wife, except it be for fornication, and shall marry another, committeth adultery: and whoso marrieth her which is put away doth commit adultery. ¹⁰His disciples say unto him, If the case of the man be so with his wife, it is not good to marry. ¹¹But he said unto them, All men cannot receive this saying, save they to whom it is *given.* ¹²*For there are some eunuchs, which were so born from their mother's womb: and there are some eunuchs, which were made eunuchs of men: and there be eunuchs, which have made themselves eunuchs for the kingdom of heaven's sake. He that is able to receive it, let him receive it."* (Matthew 19:3–12)

On two occasions in this passage, Jesus used the words *"at the beginning"* or *"from the beginning."* The beginning is an important part of what Jesus Christ believes.

■ **Marriage, divorce, and remarriage have always been matters of great dispute among Christians and all people.**

As I mentioned in the introduction, that debate still rages and will continue to rage; therefore, the Christian must search the Word of God for answers.

■ **Jesus taught the principle of original intent.**

John 1 starts, *"In the beginning was the Word...."* The Word frequently refers to the beginning because the beginning is where God established His principles and His beliefs for all that man should believe and follow. The Word, Who is the Word, Who wrote the Word, and Who knows the Word because He authored the Word was saying, "Let's go back to the beginning and see what the original intention of God was when He created the first man and the first woman."

God's original intent for marriage can be found in Genesis 2:23 and 24, which says, *"And Adam said, This is now bone of my bones, and flesh of my flesh: she shall be called Woman, because she was taken out of Man. 24Therefore shall a man leave his father and his mother, and shall cleave unto his wife: and they shall be one flesh."*

Original intent regarding marriage reveals several important principles to consider.

God's Original Intent:
One Correct Spouse in Marriage.

The original intent of God is one correct spouse created by God—a divinely preferred spouse. From how many possible spouses did Adam and Eve have to choose? God is setting a precedent and establishing a principle after which all of mankind should pattern itself—leaving and cleaving. Marriage is two people—a husband and a wife. Originally, God chose one wife for one husband. God's original intent was to bring the woman to the man. Adam did not have to go on a "woman hunt"; God brought Eve to Adam. God worked out all of the needed details. Adam's only choice was the eligible one—the only woman in the whole world. The woman, who would later receive the name Eve, was the right one for Adam.

The principle to understand is that God has a divinely preferred person for every person—and to those who are married, your divinely preferred person is the one to whom you are married. I have heard all kinds of excuses and statements, including "I know that the one I should have married was the one I dated steadily in high school but didn't marry." The "should haves" and "could haves" and "would haves" no doubt could fill a very large volume; however, that unwritten book would only contain all the sour-grapes stories of people who do not want to follow Bible principles.

So who is God's perfect will for Jack Schaap? The obvious answer is the one to whom I am married! The one to whom I said, "I do"! I am frequently asked, "Do you think people ever make mistakes in marriage?" Instead of asking that question, why not ask, "Do you ever think people make mistakes?" Of course! People make mistakes in every area of life.

Original intent does not mean that people will not violate that principle. Original intent is merely how God wants us to look at issues originally. The question is, if you want to think like God thinks, then in the case of marriage, start thinking, "There is only one person for me to marry because there is one perfect will of God for me."

Young people often ask the question, "How will I know that person who is the perfect will of God for me?" I tell them to stay in the will of God today and pray that the person they are supposed to marry will stay in the will of God; when the two meet in the proper timing, their God-given authorities will give their stamp of approval.

God's Original Intent:
Marriage Is a Spiritual and a Physical Union.

Original intent teaches that marriage is a spiritual union as well as a physical union. This spiritual union represents the spiritual teachings about Christ and salvation.

God's Original Intent:
Marriage Is the Creation of a New Family Nucleus.

Original intent teaches that marriage requires the creation of a new family nucleus, which therefore demands separation from parents. Marriage is the dissolution of the family *integrity* [wholeness]. It is the loss of the integrity to one unit so that it can divide and begin a new family unit. Marriage is a leaving and a cleaving that demands separation from parents.

Parents must realize that as soon as the new baby comes home from the hospital, the separation has begun. A very gradual, almost imperceptible separation begins as soon as the umbilical cord is cut. Over the course of time, that separation accelerates and reaches a point where the child becomes a unique adult with a distinct and individual personhood. These adults are to be treated and recognized as distinct individuals who are a reward and a heritage; they are not a parent's personal property or possession.

Children are weapons who are likened to arrows—

an offensive weapon that is only of value when it is taken from the quiver and released by means of a bow. An arrow stored in the quiver or nocked in the bow does no good. Arrows (children) are designed to go where the bow (parents) cannot go and to be launched beyond the reach of the bow. God's design for children is that they do more than their parents and that they build on their parents' foundation. Parents are like the bow and the string, and the children are like the arrows. Together the parents can combine their efforts to launch them and release them. For an arrow to be an effective offensive weapon, it must be released.

> *A marriage* is not a joining of two worlds, but an abandoning of two worlds in order that one new one might be formed.
> –Mike Mason

On the wedding day, a father escorts his daughter down the aisle on his arm, physically places her arm in the arm of his soon-to-be son-in-law, and then sits down. The father's sitting down is a symbolic statement that says, "I have completed my task." That task is likened to Christ's finished work on the Cross; it was finished. At the marriage altar, parents have completed the purpose for which God gave them a child.

Being prepared
for your wedding
≠
being prepared
for your marriage.
–Parrott

In Genesis 2:24 the clause *"they shall be one flesh"* modifies or strengthens or explains the phrase *"shall cleave unto his wife."* The husband and wife cleave and become one flesh. This Hebrew word *dabaq* meaning "welding together, a tightly cementing together," is the word chosen by God to mean not only a union of two becoming one flesh, but also speaks of a spiritual love relationship. Dr. Ed Wheat adds some further insight to cleaving.

E ven before any sin and its resulting selfishness had entered the human race, we find three basic commands: First, when we marry, we should stop being dependent on our parents or our in-laws. We are to become completely dependent on our mates to satisfy all our needs. Second, the man is the one who is responsible for holding the marriage together by "cleaving" to his wife. **Cleaving** in this sense means to be welded inseparably, so that each becomes a part of the other. Therefore, the man is to be totally

committed to his wife. Third, we are com-
manded to be joined together in sexual union,
to be **one flesh**.[1]

From the beginning, man has done his very best to
destroy God's original intent. From the beginning, Scripture unfolds about marriage, starting in Genesis with a
relatively simple analysis of what marriage is in God's
mind: one man and one woman whose divine destiny is
appointed by God, leaving family, coming together in a
union of physical oneness and a union of spiritual oneness, and starting a brand-new family. Scripture continues to unfold in Deuteronomy and Malachi. Scripture
continues to unfold in the New Testament in Matthew,
Luke, and I Corinthians 7. The Scripture has had to unfold more and more as God has had to deal with all of
man's exceptions and excuses and sin.

Parents who teach their children from the beginning that God has chosen one person for him (or her)
eliminate the need to date many members of the opposite gender. Do I think that dating many people is
wicked or sinful? No; however, I do believe that dating
can develop into somewhat of a habit. I personally believe that polygamous dating often does not breed

monogamous marriage. No, I cannot give a Scripture verse that validates that statement, but I am making that statement because I have counseled couples for 34 years. Not much is written about dating in the Bible. Some might conclude that Boaz and Ruth dated, but many Bible scholars also believe Boaz was 80 and Ruth was 40. Some might assert that Jacob dated Rachel for 14 years. Imagine today's young people following that example! I counsel with young couples in love who are agonizing over their parents' asking them to wait an extra six months—a mere 13 years and 6 months less than Jacob had to wait!

Dating is relatively a Western society social activity. I am not trying to change all the mores of society; my goal is to apply Biblical principles to life's decisions. The Bible gave man a relatively simple plan for finding a life's mate. For this reason, parents must take every available opportunity to pump values and principles into their children when they are young. Parents must start saturating their children's thinking with the idea that in the right time and at the right place, there will be a mature, hard-working, wonderful young man or young lady who is God's perfect plan for them. The right kind of teaching comes from following God's original intent—that God has one man and one woman designated by Him for each other.

God's Original Intent:
Marriage Is Ordained by God.

Marriage should not be broken by man since it is ordained by God. Jesus said, *"...What therefore God hath joined together, let not man put asunder."* (Matthew 19:6) That verse automatically gives rise to multiple questions. Fortunately, the Scripture covers all the "what-about" situations of life. The Bible is a Book of principles, and it is important to learn those principles in order to apply them in all situations of life.

■ God's mercy and love and wisdom made provision for man's failures.

Studying the cultures of man reveals the areas where man has failed and lends an understanding of how and why men have failed. Men failed in the institution of marriage in the area of adultery. Men and women began to step outside the boundaries of their marriage to engage in illicit behavior with other people's spouses or with single people in an effort to recapture their single years. A perversion of adultery is the practice of bigamy or polygamy, which legalizes adultery with another marriage ceremony. All of these examples are a violation of the original intent. *"And said, For this cause shall a man leave father and mother, and shall cleave to his wife: and they twain shall be one flesh?"* (Matthew 19:5) The words *"they twain"* eliminate adultery, bigamy, and polygamy, as well as all the nonsense of people who want to live a communal lifestyle.

Basically, God puts up with all those who do not understand or seem to grasp original intent. People will keep making unwise decisions and face failures. Thankfully, God will continue to be merciful and loving and will make provision for people's failures.

Every parent and teacher needs to learn that wonderful principle of always making provision for the failures of their followers. The Christian who learns to apply this principle of mercy will become a far more gracious person because he is choosing a higher path. Making provision for the failure of others is exactly what God did. His Son, Jesus Christ, was the Lamb slain because God, in His kindness, knew that sinful man would not obey. God then made provision for the failures of men so they could still live in relative peace with each other.

People who make terrible choices would love to have someone be merciful to them. From Christ we learn the attribute of mercy. Because God made provision for man's failure in the area of marriage, Moses wrote Deuteronomy chapter 24, which Jesus addressed in Matthew 19 in reference to the so-called rules for divorce.

"When a man hath taken a wife, and married her, and it come to pass that she find no favour in his eyes, because he hath found some uncleanness in her: then let him write her a bill of divorcement, and give it in her hand, and send her out of his house. ²And when she is departed out of his house, she may go and be another man's wife. ³And if the latter husband hate her, and write her a bill of divorcement, and giveth it in her hand, and sendeth her out of his house; or if the latter husband die, which took her to be his wife; ⁴Her former husband, which sent her away,

MARRIAGE, DIVORCE, & REMARRIAGE

may not take her again to be his wife, after that she is defiled; for that is abomination before the LORD: *and thou shalt not cause the land to sin, which the* LORD *thy God giveth thee for an inheritance."* (Deuteronomy 24:1–4)

The commandments Moses wrote regarding divorce involved divorce being allowed for moral or ceremonial (religious) or personal uncleanness. In the Jews' various theology schools, the established code of law that the people followed was the Hillel family of law—the legal jurisprudence of Jewish law. The following list contains several judicial reasons why a man could bring his wife to a court of Judaic law and be granted a divorce. According to Hillel law, each of the following explanations was a legitimate ground for being granted a divorce:

- A woman's uncovering her head
- A woman's spinning around outside and exposing any portion of flesh while showing off
- A woman's washing in a bath that is reserved for men only
- A woman's baring her arms

MARRIAGE, DIVORCE, & REMARRIAGE

- A woman's wearing slits in her dress
- A woman's talking to every man she sees
- A woman's speaking with a noisy voice and refusing to be quiet
- A woman's joking with the young men
- A woman who has any diseases in her body
- A woman who has any blemishes or warts
- A woman who has any disagreeable body odors, such as bad breath

If a husband simply looked at his wife and said, "You are no longer attractive to me" because that wife had no favor in her husband's eyes, that husband could be granted a divorce.

Once married, the woman was not all that secure [in her marriage]. She could easily be divorced. The governing text for divorce is the opening verse for Deuteronomy 24. A man may divorce his wife if "he finds in her something indecent." The followers of Hillel would accept any reason, however trivial, such as the charge that a wife had cooked a dish badly, or merely that the husband preferred another woman.[2]

Please note that none of these reasons noted by the husband included adultery because under Judaic law, adultery was punishable by death. In cases of adultery, the couple did not get divorced; if a wife was found guilty of adultery, she was executed. The uncleanness noted in Deuteronomy 24:1 and 2 only addressed the permissible reasons to divorce according to Hillel.

Jesus explained the bottom line motivator in this statement: *"...Why did Moses then command to give a writing of divorcement, and to put her away? He saith unto them, Moses because of **the hardness of your hearts** suffered you to put away your wives...."* (Matthew 19:7, 8) Jesus was saying, "If your wife does something to embarrass you or is careless about her personal hygiene, you are allowed to divorce her by official judicial law. But you and I both know the real reason is that you have a stubborn, hard heart." A husband's unwillingness to patiently work through any issues with his wife is why he chooses to divorce his spouse.

No marriage—no matter how good—is immune to bad things. We all suffer private problems and sometimes public pitfalls. Sexual unfulfillment that quietly hardens our heart. Financial debt that shrouds us in shame. Hope deferred by the anguish of infertility. Ugly addictions that drive us into secret lives. Communication meltdowns that tempt us to quit trying. Problems with anger that cause loved ones to walk on eggshells. Personal pain from an abusive past that keeps us from loving in the present. The list could go on and on. The bad things, both big and small, that interfere with a good marriage are countless.

The inevitable bad things in life that come between two loving people don't have to harm their marriage. The very opposite can be true: that bad things are to a marriage what cold water is to burning metal; it strengthens, tempers, intensifies, but does not destroy it.[3]

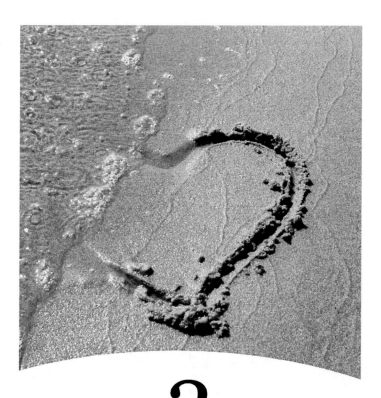

2

The Law
& DIVORCE

Love is the greatest of teachers,
for there is no authority more compelling,
no power more hypnotically transfixing,
no counsel more wise,
no message we are more longing to hear,
no other master for whom it is easier
to give up absolutely nothing
in order to follow and obey.

– Mason

This chapter will be an almost exclusive look at verses in what is commonly called the Law—the first five books of the Bible. Before addressing what the Law says about divorce, I want to look at three New Testament Scriptures that define the Law.

- Galatians 5:14 says, *"For **all the law** is fulfilled in one word, even in this; Thou shalt love thy neighbour as thyself."* *Law* is the same word Jesus used when He said in Matthew 5:17, *"Think not that I am come to destroy the law, or the prophets: I am not come to destroy, but to fulfil."* The Apostle Paul penned that **all** of the Law is fulfilled when a man loves his neighbor as himself.

- Romans 13:8–10 says, *"Owe no man any thing, but to love one another: **for he that loveth another hath fulfilled** [filled it full] **the law.** [9]For this, Thou shalt not commit adultery, Thou shalt not kill, Thou shalt not steal, Thou shalt not bear false witness, Thou shalt not covet; and if there be any other commandment, it is briefly comprehended in this saying, namely, Thou shalt love thy neighbour as thyself. [10]Love worketh no ill to*

his neighbour: therefore love is the fulfilling of the law."
This passage teaches that love fulfills—fills it full, completes it, satisfies it, overwhelms it, runs over—the Law.
Simply stated, love is the fulfilling of the Law.

• Matthew 22:35–40, *"Then one of them, which was a lawyer, asked him a question, tempting him, and saying, ³⁶Master, which is the great commandment in the law? ³⁷Jesus said unto him, Thou shalt love the Lord thy God with all thy heart, and with all thy soul, and with all thy mind. ³⁸This is the first and great commandment. ³⁹And the second is like unto it, Thou shalt love thy neighbour as thyself. ⁴⁰**On these two commandments hang all the law and the prophets."** In his book *Sacred Marriage,* author Gary Thomas shares his thoughts about the culmination of a Christian's truly loving God:

    Someone once asked Jesus what the greatest commandment was, and Jesus replied that there are two (Matthew 22:34–40). It wasn't enough to love God with all your heart, soul, mind, and strength. If you really wanted to please God, Jesus said you must love others.[1]

THE LAW AND DIVORCE

What do these three New Testament passages have to do with the Law? Very simply, the Law helps man to understand love. An individual cannot and will not understand love unless he understands the Law of God. Therefore, studying the Law will help a Christian to better understand the mind of God. The Law shows Christians a practical demonstration of love. The Law teaches Christians how God thinks on any subject matter.

I personally want to know how God thinks about a certain subject before I start telling people what I think because my thinking is sometimes polluted by a social custom or by bad teaching and training or by the pressures and coercion of life or even by my own bias toward people I love, and yes, against people whom I believe are unkind. That is why every Christian needs to study carefully and seek to understand God's thinking on matters of life.

Leviticus 21:1, *"And the LORD said unto Moses, Speak unto the priests the sons of Aaron, and say unto them…."* Everything that is written in chapter 21 addressed the priests because God intended that the integrity and respect of a priest's position be preserved. Verse 13 continues, *"And he shall take a wife in her vir-*

MARRIAGE, DIVORCE, & REMARRIAGE

ginity. ¹⁴*A widow, or a divorced woman, or profane, or an harlot, these shall he not take: but he shall take a virgin of his own people to wife."* A priest was allowed to marry only an Israeli young lady and, more specifically and preferably, a Levite who had never been defiled— a pure, upright girl. A priest could not marry a divorcee. That requirement implies that non-priests were allowed to marry divorced people.

When people ask me if I think divorced people can ever remarry, I say, "Yes." I believe the Bible teaches that remarriage is possible; however, the Scripture does say that remarriage depends on many circumstances.

The topic of divorce is complicated because there are no simple answers to divorce except for a couple to stay married once they get married. By understanding and following that one simple answer, a couple will never have to worry about any of the other resulting complications. Because I am a pastor and because many people choose not to follow God's simple first admonition, then I must know and understand what God says about divorce and remarriage.

The purpose of the Law (or the Bible) is never to use it as leverage against someone or to say, "I told you

THE LAW AND DIVORCE

so." The purpose of the Bible is to see God's perspective on the matters and issues of life. In the matter of marriage, divorce, and remarriage, God has multiple layers of what He will countenance, what He will allow, and what He will permit.

Though God is an absolute God of right and wrong, He does not have absolute demands. God does not say, "If you don't such-and-such in this one way, then I will never put up with you again." No! God puts up with all of us every day in unbelievable ways. It is only because of God's mercies that we are not consumed. Great is His faithfulness!

Leviticus 22:13 says, *"But if the priest's daughter be a widow, or divorced, and have no child, and is returned unto her father's house, as in her youth, she shall eat of her father's meat: but there shall no stranger eat thereof."* Again, this verse teaches some principles of how God thinks and how Christians are to form a basis for making principled decisions to use in working with people.

In Leviticus 22:13, a priest's daughter had married, and her husband had died or they had divorced, and the couple had no children. The implication of this verse, not the clear expression, is that if she had had a child, she could not or should not move back to her parents' home; rather, she should maintain the integrity of the unit of her home. If she had no child, the implication seems to be that she can move back in with her parents and once again be under their authority. I find this verse very interesting because sometimes in working with couples who are divorcing, I believe the wife is totally justified in allowing her father to make some decisions in her life. I have even counseled fathers that once the divorce is definite, he may need to take over and bring his daughter home under his roof.

I have also told divorced women with children who wanted to move home that they might retreat there temporarily, but they could not live there permanently. I explain that they must eventually have their own home because a family needs to remain intact. When I am asked to explain that thinking and reasoning, some people say, "That is Old Testament Law." The same God Who wrote the New Testament also wrote the Old Testament, and these verses show God's perspective on the home and marriage.

In Leviticus 22:13, both the widow and the divorced were named side by side. Numbers 30:9 says, *"But every*

THE LAW AND DIVORCE

vow of a widow, and of her that is divorced...." These two categories—widows and divorced—come under almost identical principles. The Bible teaches believers to treat a divorced person with the same kind of care, concern, respect, and deference given to a widow. Numerous times in the Bible they are listed together; and since God records them together and often holds them to the same principles, so must we. The divorced person should not bear a stigma for the divorce.

Deuteronomy 22:13, 14, *"If any man take a wife, and go in unto her, and hate her, ¹⁴And give occasions of speech against her, and bring up an evil name upon her, and say, I took this woman, and when I came to her, I found her not a maid."* If a man marries a woman but from the beginning does not like her because he doubts her purity, the husband may make public statements against her and impugn her character.

The passage continues, *"Then shall the father of the damsel, and her mother, take and bring forth the tokens of the damsel's virginity unto the elders of the city in the gate: ¹⁶And the damsel's father shall say unto the elders, I gave my daughter unto this man to wife, and he hateth her; ¹⁷And, lo, he hath given occasions of speech against her, saying, I found not thy daughter a maid; and yet these are the tokens of my daughter's virginity. And they shall spread the cloth before the elders of the city. [18]And the elders of that city shall take that man and chastise him; [19]And they shall amerce* [give; to punish by a fine] *him in an hundred shekels of silver, and give them unto the father of the damsel, because he hath brought up an evil name upon a virgin of Israel: and she shall be his wife; he may not put her away all his days."* When a husband accuses his wife of already being impure when they were married, a legal process begins. She and her parents go to the elders (judges) of the city and announce their intention to prove that their daughter was pure. After all, that accusation has hurt the character and reputation of the wife as well as her family. If the proof given meets the satisfaction of those in authority, that husband may never divorce his wife for any reason whatsoever.

Deuteronomy 22:13–19 takes precedence over Deuteronomy 24, which says that if a man finds some uncleanness in his spouse, he can give her a writing of divorcement. She must then leave his house, and she may become another man's wife. Woe be to the man who desecrates the testimony of a pure young lady! If a man accuses his wife of wrongdoing, slanders her name, and assassinates her testimony of purity and if his accusation is proven unfounded, he may never divorce his wife for any reason.

Deuteronomy 22:28 and 29 share yet another facet of God's mind about the subject of marriage, divorce, and remarriage. *"If a man find a damsel that is a virgin, which is not betrothed* [not engaged or has no legal document to marry], *and lay hold on her, and lie with her, and they be found;* [29]*Then the man that lay with her shall give unto the damsel's father fifty shekels of silver, and she shall be his wife; because he hath humbled her, he may not put her away all his days."*

The Biblical precedent for intimate behavior before marriage carried a penalty of never being allowed to divorce the person for any reason whatsoever. In Bible days, premarital intimacy was worthy of death; however, God spared the couple of the death penalty. Instead, the Law decreed that the couple marry; the guilty man pay the girl's father a hefty fine; and then they could never divorce.

MARRIAGE, DIVORCE, & REMARRIAGE

Originally the law (Exodus 22:15–17) stated that in the case of sexual relations with an unmarried woman, the man was forced to pay the value of the daughter to the father. The father then had the option of forcing the man to marry the daughter or not. The reform in Deuteronomy 22:25–27 stated that once the fifty shekels were paid to the father, there was no choice. The man had to marry the woman and was not permitted to divorce her.[2]

The young man was given no choice in the matter because he had spoiled the young lady's purity. I find that the number-one way a young man takes a young lady's purity is by persuading her to prove her love through intimacy. According to the Bible, forcing her to prove that love means he can never put her away. Following Old Testament Law to the letter would mean that 80 percent of married couples may never get divorced.

Jeremiah 3:6–8, *"The Lord said also unto me in the days of Josiah the king, Hast thou seen that which backsliding Israel hath done? she is gone up upon every high mountain and under every*

*green tree, and there hath played the harlot
[prostitute]. ⁷And I said after she had done all
these things, Turn thou unto me. But she returned
not.... ⁸And I saw, when for all the causes whereby
backsliding Israel committed adultery I had put
her away, and given her a bill of divorce...."*

Isaiah 50:1 records the same identical story. In Exodus 19 and 20, Jehovah God married the nation of Israel at Mt. Sinai. The phrase at the beginning of Exodus 20:2 which says, *"I am the LORD thy God,"* is a marriage covenant or vow that God made to Israel, His chosen nation. To God Israel replied, *"...All that the LORD hath spoken we will do...."* (Exodus 19:8) Once the marriage vows were spoken, God and His

A covenant is not like a modern contract in which people confront each other with different sets of obligations. In the contract, if one of the parties fails, then the contract is voided. By contrast the covenant between Israel and God was a generous bonding initiated by God. He accepted Israel despite its continued unfaithfulness. This is the sense of commitment which had its impact on the thinking of marriage in the Old Testament.³

people entered into a marriage covenant. Imagine God's heartbreak when He wrote a bill of divorcement to Israel. God, the ultimate Priest, had married the nation of Israel. However, the nation played the harlot on God. Still, God did not divorce the nation for a one-time transgression or even for several times.

Only after Israel's repeated transgressing did God finally respond in Jeremiah 3:8, *"And I saw, when for all the causes whereby backsliding Israel committed adultery I had put her away...."* All the causes are explained in the last part of verse 6, *"...she is gone up upon every high mountain and under every green tree, and there hath played the harlot."* Because Israel repeatedly committed spiritual adultery, God divorced Israel.

> *C*ommitment is the mortar that holds the stones of marriage in place.
> –Parrott

If a husband believes his wife has had an affair and he wants a divorce, he can obtain a divorce if her infidelity involves one of the reasons that the Hillel court of Judaism approved for a couple to divorce. However, if that husband wants to adopt God's thinking, he will still want his wife—no matter how many affairs his wife has. For the multiple times His bride Israel played the adulteress, God still wanted His people to come back to Him. Only after numerous rejections did God finally consent to write a bill of divorce.

> *"O Israel, return unto the LORD thy God; for thou hast fallen by thine iniquity. [2]Take with you words [your marriage vows], and turn to the LORD: say unto him, Take away all iniquity, and receive us graciously: so will we render the calves of our lips. [3]Asshur shall not save us; we will not ride upon horses: neither will we say any more to the work of our hands, Ye are our gods: for in thee the fatherless findeth mercy. [4]I will heal their backsliding, I will love them freely: for mine anger is turned away from him. [5]I will be as the dew unto Israel: he shall grow as the lily, and cast forth his roots as Lebanon. [6]His branches shall spread, and his beauty shall be as the olive tree, and his smell as Lebanon. [7]They that dwell under his shadow shall return; they shall revive as the corn, and grow as the vine: the scent thereof shall be as the wine of Lebanon. [8]Ephraim shall say,*

MARRIAGE, DIVORCE, & REMARRIAGE
✒

What have I to do any more with idols? I have heard him, and observed him: I am like a green fir tree. From me is thy fruit found. ⁹Who is wise, and he shall understand these things? prudent, and he shall know them? for the ways of the LORD are right, and the just shall walk in them: but the transgressors shall fall therein." (Hosea 14:1–9)

The entire book of Hosea is an illustration of a prophet's marriage to a woman who would be unfaithful to him. God told His prophet Hosea to put away his adulterous wife Gomer for a period of time, and eventually Hosea would remarry her. Hosea was a picture of Jehovah God; Gomer pictured the nation of Israel. When Gomer went into harlotry just like the nation of Israel did, God told Hosea to put her away (divorce her) as a means to bring her back. In other words, God divorced Israel as a tool to provoke her to come back— not as a means of eliminating a problem.

God did not find someone else to marry! God remarried Israel because He did not want anyone else. The descriptive language God uses (which is very similar to the language of the Song of Solomon) beautifully illustrates God and a nation re-entering the covenant of romance, love, and marriage. God did divorce Israel because of a lifestyle of multiple adulteries—not because of a bad day. He only divorced her to provoke her to come back. Hosea's wife gave birth to illegitimate children, and Hosea even went so far as to take her children and rear them as his own. When Gomer was no longer wanted or desired by anyone, God brought her back to Hosea, and the family was finally reunited. The book of Hosea is a storybook picture illustrating how God feels about Israel.

People state in all certainty that God hates divorce. No! God hates all the causes and all the reasons that provoke divorce. In God's mind, divorce can be a tool to provoke an offending spouse to return to his/her marriage. To be sure divorcing for that reason is a high-risk move. As a matter of fact, it is such a high-risk move that I do not recommend it because I am not God. In rare instances, I do recommend temporary separation. God had already written the book of Hosea, and He knew from the beginning that divorce would provoke her to come back.

MARRIAGE, DIVORCE, & REMARRIAGE

I personally do not recommend divorce as a matter of principle; but when I see it happening, I pray that the divorce will be used as a provocation to remarry. One of the most important lessons that the Apostle Paul writes about divorce is not to rush into another marriage because the preeminent thought of the person who has just divorced should be, "Could God use this ending to revive our dead marriage?"

The principle of marriage is a spiritual institution, and all spiritual institutions operate on spiritual laws. The spiritual law is the death, the burial, and the resurrection; it is a Calvary principle, if you please. *"…Except a corn of wheat fall into the ground and die, it abideth alone: but if it die, it bringeth forth much fruit."* (John 12:24) What does this verse mean in relation to marriage and divorce?

Some marriages must die before they can resurrect and have a blossoming, fruitful marriage. That is why God chose a term like *fruitful* to describe marriage. *"Thy wife shall be as a fruitful vine by the sides of thine house: thy children like olive plants round about thy table."* (Psalm 128:3) The marriage went dead for a period of time; but with the demonstration of faithful-

THE LAW AND DIVORCE

ness and love, the marriage came back together, even though divorce was used as a tool to resurrect it.

> *Reconciliation* is paved with words of kindness.
> –Gary Chapman

If divorce is a way for a person to quickly run into the arms of someone who has been waiting in the wings, then that individual has no concept of what godliness is. One's goal must be redemption and reconciliation— not someone else.

Matthew 1 is still under the Law even though the book of Matthew is in the New Testament; it is Old Testament until the Cross. Matthew 1:18 and 19, *"Now the birth of Jesus Christ was on this wise: When as his mother Mary was espoused* [The couple had not lived together, but they had a contractual agreement] *to Joseph, before they came together, she was found with child of the Holy Ghost. Then Joseph her husband, being a just man, and not willing to make her a publick example, was minded to put her away privily."* To understand the deeper meaning of this Scripture, Deuteronomy 22 must be considered.

Deuteronomy 22:23 and 24 says, *"If a damsel* [a young lady] *that is a virgin be betrothed* [espoused or engaged] *unto an husband, and a man find her in the city, and lie with her;* [24]*Then ye shall bring them both out unto the gate of that city* [city hall, not the city limits], *and ye shall stone them with stones that they die; the damsel, because she cried not, being in the city; and the man, because he hath humbled his neigbour's wife: so thou shalt put away evil from among you."* This young lady, who is legally espoused to someone else, is defiled by another man.

The laws governing extramarital relations and rape are helping in realizing the importance put upon a woman's fidelity. If a married woman was found to have had relations with another man willingly, she was to be put to death. When a rape of a married woman or one betrothed took place within the city walls, both the woman and the man committing the crime were to be stoned. The man's fault was that he did not respect the rights of another family. The woman's fault was that she did not resist with her very being when there was a possibility that the attack could have been overheard and stopped. If, however, the rape took place in the country, only the man would be executed since there was little hope that the woman in her distress could be heard by others.[4]

I have no doubt that when Joseph discovered Mary was expecting, he was thinking about the possibility of a public stoning of Mary; and I have no doubt he was considering the letter of the Law in Deuteronomy 22 in regard to Mary's being an expectant mother. Joseph had two options:

- If he took Mary to city hall, she would be stoned.
- If he found any manner of uncleanness in Mary, he could write her a bill of divorcement and send her out of his life.

The justice is that Joseph chose the more honorable way for his wife. Technically, the word *betrothed* in the Bible is nearly the same as having a wife. Because a legal document had been signed, Joseph had a difficult choice to make. Joseph loved Mary and did not want to make her a public example. Even as he was choosing the lesser of the two options, the angel of the Lord came to him and told Joseph that Mary was carrying a child conceived by the Holy Ghost. Then Joseph did his husbandly duty by taking Mary to live with him, though they did not live together as husband and wife until after the birth of Jesus. Joseph chose fairness and justice and kindness instead of destruction and death. The Law is illustrating what love is. I like what Gary Chapman says about love: "Love is the attitude that exalts the interests of the other person."[5] Most assuredly, Joseph had Mary's best interest at heart.

God divorced Israel because He loved her so much He wanted her back; and after much pleading, He gave in and divorced His beloved nation. When I am counseling a troubled marriage, I advise the couple to have great patience—like God. When a spouse is playing the fool, being very kind and very patient will eventually cause the offending spouse to wake up to his betrayal and realize the error of his way. When patience and kindness are exercised, many times couples are reunited. That reuniting is why the Law gives options, and that is what love is. Love is the fulfilling of the Law.

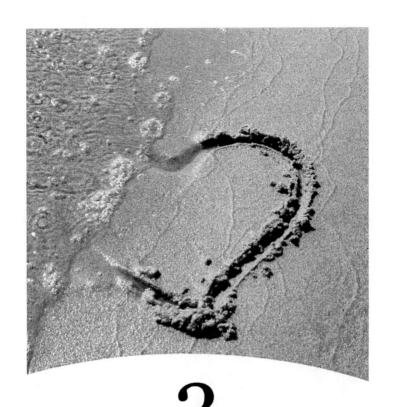

3
Jesus on
MARRIAGE,
DIVORCE, & REMARRIAGE

Love the Lord thy God...love thy neighbour...
Christ certainly knew what He was doing
when He joined those two commandments together.
The ability to love others is totally dependent
on our ability to love Him. The more completely
we love Him, the more balanced and complete
our love for others will be.

– Smalley

This chapter will address what I believe are probably the strongest Scriptures on the subject of marriage, divorce, and remarriage. The strongest Scriptures concerning marriage, divorce, and remarriage come from the lips of Jesus Christ, and no individual has been, is, or ever will be stronger on any issue than Jesus Christ. Matthew 5:17 and 18 says, *"Think not that I am come to destroy the law, or the prophets: I am not come to destroy, but to fulfil. ¹⁸For verily I say unto you, Till heaven and earth pass, one jot or one tittle shall in no wise pass from the law, till all be fulfilled."*

In Matthew 5 Jesus is defining and fulfilling the Law. *Fulfilling* means "filling it up full." I liken this definition to a patron's drinking a cup of coffee at a restaurant. When his cup is about half full, a watchful waitress will notice and ask, "Would you like me to fill it up?" When the waitress refills the cup, please note that the waitress hasn't changed the contents of the cup at all; she just filled it full—fulfilled it. Practically speaking, that is what Jesus said about the Law. He did not come to change the contents of the Law. The waitress did not add lemonade to the coffee; she came to fill it up full and reheat the coffee. Jesus is doing the same; He is going to "heat things up" and fill up the Law—not change it.

Jesus was adding the qualities of love and heart and soul to the Law. Without a firm or complete understanding, the Law seems harsh, a little sterile, and even unfeeling and uncompassionate. Jesus is adding an emotional dimension, intention, and meaning to the Law. Jesus is giving man a perspective of the Law that is not seen in just reading the Old Testament; therefore, man is receiving Jesus' fuller understanding. The concept of marriage and divorce and remarriage is growing and building in the Scriptures; none of it contradicts. Rather, it expands in its understanding. Jesus is bringing some moral understanding to the Law.

Jesus added motive and intention to the commandments of the Law. A person's motives and intentions help to discern and define the interpretation of his behavior. It is not simply a matter of asking, "Did you or did you not do thus and so?" Rather, the question to ask is, "Why did you do thus and so, and what were your intentions?"

JESUS ON MARRIAGE, DIVORCE,...

Our very gracious God is willing to look at man's motives and intentions. God is not machine-like; He does not make every person exactly alike. His desire to see the intention fills up the Law a little fuller.

Jesus taught that man's understanding of the Law is incomplete without the further revelation that He provided. Psalm 119:18 says, *"Open thou mine eyes, that I may behold wondrous things out of thy law."* David was asking God to open his understanding to the Law. The Psalmist knew he could read the words of God; but unless he possessed God's understanding, David knew he would miss the full meaning in those words. Likewise, a Christian needs to hear what the Spirit is saying while he is reading the Words that God wrote.

Regarding marriage and divorce and remarriage, Jesus taught that the seventh commandment is the foundation for interpretation concerning divorce. The full meaning of divorce is found in Exodus 20:14, which states, *"Thou shalt not commit adultery."*

Obviously, the word *divorce* is not found in Matthew 5, but Jesus' teaching about divorce is based upon that commandment. Not to understand that commandment is to miss Jesus' teaching about whether or not divorce is right or wrong or anything in-between. Six times in Matthew 5, Jesus "fills up" the Law:

- Matthew 5:21, 22: "*Ye have heard that it was said by them of old time, Thou shalt not kill...* ***But I say unto you....*"* Obviously, "*Thou shalt not kill*" is one of the Ten Commandments.

- Matthew 5:27, 28: "*Ye have heard that it was said by them of old time, Thou shalt not commit adultery:* ***But I say unto you....*"*

- Matthew 5:31, 32: "*It hath been said,...****But I say unto you....*"*

- Matthew 5:33, 34: "*Again, ye have heard that it hath been said by them of old time,... **But I say unto you....*"*

- Matthew 5:38, 39: "*Ye have heard that it hath been said,...****But I say unto you....*"*

- Matthew 5:43, 44: "*Ye have heard that it hath been said,...****But I say unto you....*"*

I believe those powerful words "*But I say unto you*" really are the crux of all marriage counseling. Many times I tell a couple with whom I am counseling that I full well understand what both of them are saying and that I am on their side as human beings. However, what that couple must consider is what Jesus says. These verses in Matthew 5 reveal God's motives and His intentions; the stance Jesus was taking was even more difficult than the Law.

The Law is practical and common sense, and Jesus' fulfillment of the Law allows the Christian to see His heart. There is great purpose in man's comprehension of the Law of God. Every time Jesus spoke on divorce, He was confronting a group of people who did not want to hear what He had to say. Jesus spoke with great intention and purpose. Jesus addressed divorce in four predominate passages in the Gospels: Matthew 5, Matthew 19, Mark 10, and Luke 16. Consulting only those passages without looking at the Law and at what the Apostle Paul wrote reveals singularly the very strong stance Jesus took on the subject of divorce.

■ What Does Jesus Say About Divorce?

Adultery is not only an action of the body but also an intention of the heart. Matthew 5:27, 28, *"Ye have heard that it was said by them of old time, Thou shalt not commit adultery: But I say unto you, That whoso-*

ever looketh on a woman to lust after her hath commit-ted adultery with her already in his heart." Before ad-dressing divorce, Jesus first defined adultery. A woman who was taken in the very act (or action) of adultery was brought to Him. Jesus says that adultery is not just an action; committing adultery is also an intention. If a man looks with the intent of wanting, he has broken the Law. Jesus was drawing an even tougher line.

Adultery has severe consequences and should be avoided at any cost according to Matthew 5:29, 30 which says, *"And if thy right eye offend thee, pluck it out, and cast it from thee: for it is profitable for thee that one of thy members should perish, and not that thy whole body should be cast into hell. ³⁰And if thy right hand of-fend thee, cut it off, and cast it from thee: for it is prof-itable for thee that one of thy members should perish, and not that thy whole body should be cast into hell."*

In my study of 30-plus years, I have yet to find a commentator who believes Matthew 5:29 and 30 liter-ally. Why? In our finite human minds, Jesus' words are too radical. However, only Jesus knows how terrible Hell is. The intention of this verse is for a man to de-stroy his dominant eye rather than to lust. Frequently, the hand often takes to possess that which the eye lusts after. Achan saw the gold and the goodly Babylonish garment; he lusted and wanted the items, so he took them. The "I saw" and the "I took" often go together. Authors Allender and Longman define *lust* as:

> …the fallen desire for union gone mad. Lust may be sexual, but it may also be directed toward a person or object in a nonsexual manner. Lust may be directed toward a person, object, position, or state. Many lust after being happy (state); others lust after reputation (position), antiques (objects), or people. In any case, destructive lust involves the heart of a thief whose passion is to be satisfied, not the heart of a lover whose desire is to give.[1]

Achan lusted for objects, took them, and brought heartbreak, judgment, and condemnation to his entire family. Sadly, adultery often follows the same formula. An individual sees something he wants, so he takes and inevitably brings heartache to his family. Jesus asks the lustful person, "Why don't you render yourself incapable of doing either?"

MARRIAGE, DIVORCE, & REMARRIAGE

Some records do exist of Christians who did indeed take Jesus' words literally. However, nearly all Bible commentators agree that mutilation of the body is also forbidden in Scripture. Still, Jesus is not contradicting Himself. What Jesus is stressing is that a man had better go to any extreme to keep from committing adultery. Jesus was laying down a very strong foundation about adultery before He addressed divorce, and there is a reason for that groundwork.

Jesus' strong stance against adultery is that divorce too often follows right on the heels of an individual's committing adultery. I find the wording of Matthew 5:31 very interesting: *"It hath been said,…"* is a shortened introductory statement that appears in only one of six verses. This Scripture leaves out the words *"…of old time."* I believe that Jesus is cutting right to the chase. Jesus warns man to take whatever measures he has to in order to avoid adultery. He warns that those who commit adultery are in danger of living hell on earth.

After Jesus takes His strong stance on adultery, then He adds a "by the way" and mentions a bill of divorcement referring to Deuteronomy 24:1–4. Matthew 5:31 and 32 say, *"It hath been said, Whosoever shall put*

away his wife, let him give her a writing of divorcement:
³²But I say unto you, That whosoever shall put away [divorce] *his wife, saving* [except] *for the cause of fornication, causeth her to commit adultery: and whosoever shall marry her that is divorced committeth adultery."*
In this verse sequence, Jesus has gone from addressing adultery in Matthew 5:28 to divorce in verse 31 and back to adultery in verse 32.

Keep in mind, to understand Jesus' thoughts about divorce, Jesus had to first address the subject of adultery. About adultery, Jesus basically says to do whatever it takes to stop the intent and acting upon that intent. Adultery is an action, and adultery is also an intention.

Jesus says if a person even looks with affection and desire, he has already committed adultery in his heart. Jesus says a man should do anything to keep from committing adultery—even to taking the most extreme of measures to avoid adultery. Then Jesus adds that divorcing one's spouse for any reason can open the door to adultery. Jesus is magnifying the severity of the cause of divorce. If man knew what Jesus thought about adultery, he would never file for divorce because divorce is a legal permission. Deuteronomy 24 states a man can give his wife a bill of divorcement; she may leave the house and become another man's wife. The Law permits a person to remarry.

Matthew 5:32 introduces the phrase, *"...saving for the cause of fornication...,"* that many claim make an allowance for divorce. *Fornication* is an encompassing word meaning "any sexual sin." Used in this context, the word *fornication* refers to Jehovah God's divorcing Israel because of the nation's multiple adulteries in an effort to win back His people. The person who divorces a spouse guilty of flagrant, repetitious, wanton departure from the bounds of marriage in an effort to win the person back has the proper intentions and is acting like God. Divorce was only to be used as a last-ditch effort to provoke a spouse to return.

In counseling when divorce is proposed to me as a means of a couple's solving their problems, I generally make a common statement to them. I tell the one who is about to be divorced to make sure the lawyer knows that his/her spouse wants a divorce and to ask the divorce lawyer to sue for every possible penny and custody of the children. The party seeking the divorce will generally lose a significant portion of his income. I only make this recommendation in an effort to provoke the couple to stay together. If God says in Proverbs 13:15, *"...the way of transgressors is hard,"* I personally refuse to make it easy on a couple planning to divorce.

Within the walls of my office, I hear every imaginable reason for divorce. Commonly, and so many times I cannot count them, I hear the words, "I never loved him/her." I agree wholeheartedly with what the author, Gary Thomas, asserts in his book *Sacred Marriage*:

> Put in a Christian context, saying "I've never loved you" is a confession of the man's utter failure to be a Christian. If he hasn't loved his wife, it is not his wife's fault, but his. Jesus calls us to love the unlovely—even our enemies—so a man who says, "I've never loved you" is a man who is saying essentially this: I've never acted like a Christian."[2]

When a couple claims incompatibility or that they no longer love each other and decides to divorce on those grounds, they are routinely giving each other permission to commit adultery. Furthermore, they are giving permission to anyone who marries them to commit adultery. In such a case, who receives the blame for those cases of adultery? The person who initiates the divorce receives the blame for his adultery, his ex-spouse's adultery, and the adultery of the person who marries his ex-spouse. Jesus was very tough on the matter of adultery.

Unless the cause for the divorce was the immoral behavior of the spouse, then there is no legal permission to remarry. Matthew 19:3, 4, 8, *"The Pharisees also came unto him, tempting him, and saying unto him, Is it lawful for a man to put away his wife for every cause? ⁴And he answered and said unto them, Have ye not read, that he which made them at the beginning made them male and female. ⁸He saith unto them, Moses because of the hardness of your hearts suffered you to put away your wives: but from the beginning it was not so."*

Jesus taught that His addition to the Law did not void the original purpose of the creation of the Law. In Moses' day, a written bill of divorcement meant the spouse was sent from the house. The couple could not live together after the papers were served, and that is the reason why papers are still served today. Just because Moses made that statement does not mean the original purpose was void or contradicted. In the beginning God never intended for a married couple to leave each other; Jesus reinforced that original intent in Matthew 19.

Jesus explained to the Pharisees that Moses had permitted divorce only because of their "hardness of heart" (Matthew 19:8) but that from the beginning divorce was not God's plan. Jesus affirmed that God's intention was monogamous, lifelong marital relationships. When God instituted marriage, divorce was not an option. God did not create divorce any more than He created polygamy. Those were man's innovations. In God's sight, those innovations are always clearly wrong.[3]

One who marries a divorced person also commits adultery. Matthew 19:9, *"And I say unto you, Whosoever shall put away his wife, except it be for fornication, and shall marry another, committeth adultery: and whoso marrieth her which is put away doth commit adultery."*

Jesus taught that the principle human reasoning behind all divorce was an unforgiving spirit. Jesus said in Matthew 19:8, *"...Moses because of the hardness of your hearts suffered* [allowed] *you to put away* [divorce] *your wives: but from the beginning it was not so."*

What is the ultimate reason why Moses was used by God to pen Deuteronomy 24? Deuteronomy does not reveal the reasons why Moses wrote the book, but Jesus is the One Who gave Moses the words to write, and He alone knows why He inspired those words.

Moses had been putting up with the nonsense of a stiff-necked and hardhearted people for 40 years. He led a people who rebelled consistently, and he was drained by the defiant behavior of the children of Israel. Moses wanted to put some structure to God's people choosing divorce like the heathen nations. Deuteronomy 24 structured divorce, but Jesus was saying the only reason Moses was given those words was a result of the hard, rebellious hearts of the people.

When Jesus talks about the toughness of the law of divorce, He addresses the motive and the heart, leaving out the law. The reason for people's divorcing is that they possess stubborn, hard hearts. Jesus looked at a couple and said one was stubborn and hardhearted to leave, and the other was stubborn and hardhearted not to put up with the issues. Jesus put up with sin that put Him on a cross! "Suffering is part of the Christian life, modeled by Jesus Christ Himself, who suffered immeasurably in His service to God."[4]

If Jesus could put up with the Cross, a husband and a wife can surely be patient with each other. "Divorce represents our inability to hold to Jesus' command. It's giving up on what Jesus calls us to do. Yes, this spouse might be difficult to love at times, but that's what marriage is for—to teach us how to love."[5]

Jesus taught that the principal human reason for divorce was an unforgiving spirit. "To forgive is to withhold judgment, forswear vengeance, renounce bitterness, break the silence of estrangement, and actually wish the best for the person who has hurt us. Forgiveness is not for the faint-hearted. Only the brave forgive."[6]

MARRIAGE, DIVORCE, & REMARRIAGE

Jesus was not presenting a harder line of divorce; rather, Jesus was dealing with the heart of the matter. The heart of the matter is always a hard heart that is unwilling to forgive. Jesus is saying that marriage is hard work.

When couples observe that marriage requires "work," what they mean primarily is that it takes time. They mean it robs them of precious time. Like it or not, you and your spouse are in it together and in it for life, and the work in marriage is the most vital work you can do. In the Lord's plans for the world there is no work more important than the work of relationship, and no relationship is more important than that of one's marriage.[7]

Not everyone can be as responsible in marriage as the laws of marriage demand. Matthew 19:10, 11 says, *"His disciples say unto him, If the case of the man be so with his wife, it is not good to marry. But he said unto them, All men cannot receive this saying, save they to whom it is given."* Statistics show that 52 percent of marriages end in divorce. Many people cannot handle the demands of marriage because they do not understand what marriage is. Marriage is not a stronger friendship. Marriage is not the next step after hugging and kissing. Marriage is not feeling romantic during the holiday season or feeling tender after attending a romantic banquet such as a Valentine banquet.

Marriage is an abundance of hard work. The harder a couple works at the marriage, the more likely they will have a marriage someone else would like to have— without doing the work.

> *Genuine* love: doing what is right no matter what the other person does or says
> –Gary Smalley

Marriage Is Not for Those Who Will Not Forgive.

"Forgiveness begins with a simple decision, a simple act of the will. We are to forgive as God has forgiven us. It is not dependent upon our spouse asking for our forgiveness or even acknowledging he or she has done anything wrong."[8]

Dating couple, ask yourself, "How forgiving is the person I am dating?" Young lady, if you show up ten minutes late for a date, what is his attitude like? If he

The five most important words that you can ever learn are these:
"I am proud of you."
The four most important words are:
"What do you think?
The three most important words are: **"I am sorry."**
The two most important words are: **"Forgive me."**
The single most important word in a relationship is: **"We."**[9]

says, "You better not be late again," my advice would be never to marry him!

Marriage Is Not for the Immoral.

If an unmarried couple is immoral, neither one is ready for marriage because marriage is a spiritual institution that is designed to manifest the purity of the flesh—not the immorality of the flesh. The immorality of the flesh is often evidenced by a second, a third, and a fourth marriage. Immorality is miserable glue. Being together physically before marriage is not a guarantee of staying together forever. "Sex outside the lifelong covenant of permanence and fidelity sets up expectations and creates needs that almost always dismantle the relationship."[10] Statistics show that the more a couple tries to act like a husband and wife before marriage, the less likely they will stay together as a husband and wife after marriage.

Marriage Is Not for Those Who Will Not Confine Themselves to One Person.

Marriage is being willing to give up single friends. Married men are to give up their single buddies, and married ladies are to give up their single girlfriends. "Marriage is an exclusive club. Marriage is a two-person arrangement, leaving out all other parties. That is why wedding vows include the phrase, 'forsaking all others.' "[11]

Marriage Is Not for Those Who Want an Excuse to Disobey God.

Marriage Is Not for Those Who Lack the Discipline and the Willpower to Commit to Marriage.

If you are the kind of person who is looking for an excuse and wanting to justify why you do not think God understands your condition, don't even think about falling in love and getting married! Marriage is for those who have that inflexible will which says, "I promised. I keep my word." Consider what Lawrence Crabb, Jr., asserts in his book, *The Marriage Builder*:

> If we deeply believe that the Lord is able to work on our behalf in all circumstances, then no collection of marital setbacks will prompt us to seriously consider divorce or withdrawal. If God is really as powerful as He claims to be, then the path of obedience will always lead to His intended purposes.[12]

I believe the key verses by Jesus on the subject of marriage are found in Luke 16:15-18, *"And he said unto them, Ye are they which justify yourselves before men; but God knoweth your hearts: for that which is highly esteemed among men is abomination in the sight of God. [16]The law and the prophets were until John: since that time the kingdom of God is preached, and every man presseth into it. [17]And it is easier for heaven and earth to pass, than one tittle of the law to fail. [18]Whosoever putteth away his wife, and marrieth another, committeth adultery: and whosoever marrrieth her that is put away from her husband committeth adultery."* Verse 18 is the crux of what Jesus Christ teaches on marriage.

In all truthfulness, marriage is not for the faint of heart nor for the cowardly nor for the unforgiving. Marriage is for saying goodbye to parents, family, and friends. Married couples must have a tender heart, a firm and resolute will, and a forgiving spirit.

> *Jesus* called marriage good; Scripture called it good. In fact the New Testament in Ephesians 5 links the bond of marriage in a special way with the work of Jesus in the church.
> – Thomas Martin

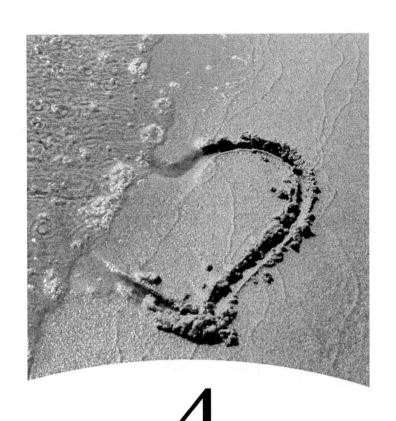

4

Paul on
MARRIAGE & REMARRIAGE

More than seeing
marriage as a mutual comfort,
we must see it as a word picture
of the most important news
humans have ever received—
that there is a divine relationship
between God and His people.
Paul explicitly makes this analogy
in his letter to the Ephesians
(Ephesians 5:25-27).

– Gary Thomas

I Corinthians 7:1, 2, *"Now concerning the things whereof ye wrote unto me: It is good for a man not to touch a woman. ²Nevertheless, to avoid fornication, let every man have his own wife, and let every woman have her own husband."*

Because the Corinthian church was under intense persecution, the Apostle Paul was giving specific advice to the Corinthian church members who were going through difficult times and much hardship. Both the Roman Empire and the Jewish community were exerting incredible pressure on these Christians. With these two great geo-political forces pressuring the church, the members wrote a letter containing questions to the Apostle Paul. "Paul had enough insight into human nature to realize that the community of believers would not go unaffected by the larger society. He appreciated the difficulty that the Christians in this community had in living a life of responsible commitment."[1]

Paul wrote a response to the Corinthians answering their questions. One of their questions dealt with the issue of divorce. In I Corinthians 7, Paul answered a question about marriage. He generally presented Scriptural information and a general understanding about marriage specifically for the Corinthian people.

In looking at marriage, divorce, and remarriage from Paul's Scriptural viewpoint, God's extended mercy toward man is evidenced. I have found that the most judgmental people about marriage, divorce, and remarriage are those who have not extensively studied the Scriptures regarding the subject.

The context of I Corinthians 6 addresses the Christian's body as being pure and belonging to God. Because the Christian's body is the temple of the Holy Ghost, he should not indulge in sexually impure behavior. Some theologians believe the context of I Corinthians 7:1 means that in order for a man to avoid fornication, he should not touch a woman. The word *touch* in the Bible is often a Greek word that is sometimes translated "simply touch," like touching an inanimate object. However, in this context of marriage in I Corinthians 7:1, the term *touch* is a much more intimate and sacred term.

In today's vernacular Paul is saying, "Are you asking me a question about whether or not it is good for a man to marry a woman?" Paul is addressing marriage because both the Roman and the Greek culture alleged that marriage was evil. The philosophers and the so-called journalists of the day wrote scathing treatises about the foolishness of getting married, so the Corinthian people were disturbed by the philosophies of the heathen cultures surrounding them. The Roman culture was crude in their vulgarity, and the Greeks were sophisticated in their vulgarity.

When Paul penned these words, he was writing to a morally corrupt Corinth that abounded with much sensual lust and sexual perversions. Paul was advising the Corinthian people to be very careful about their reasoning for marrying. Paul answered that marriage is a spiritual institution.

If a couple contemplating marriage does not want to follow the laws of God, I would advise them not to get married. The institution of marriage is not for those who believe it is time to get married simply because they are in their twenties or because of peer pressure or cultural significance or tax incentives. All of these kinds of immature reasons to marry spell d-i-v-o-r-c-e.

The Corinthians felt the pressure of their culture

MARRIAGE, DIVORCE, & REMARRIAGE

not to marry, and Paul said it was certainly acceptable not to marry. He "balances" verse 1 with verse 2, which says, *"Nevertheless, to avoid fornication, let every man have his own wife, and let every woman have her own husband."* I do not believe this verse primarily teaches that marriage is a good answer for those who are burning in their lust. Authors Allender and Longman define *lust* as "the effort to possess another in order to steal enough passion to be lifted out of our current struggles into a world that feels (for an instant) like the Garden of Eden."[2]

If a person has an addiction problem with lust, that problem will only increase after marriage. Marriage does not alter a person's lustful character; it only locks him in and ultimately causes greater frustration. Though some commentators say this verse means for single people to marry if they cannot control themselves, Paul teaches that this Scripture is addressing married people.

The Apostle Paul was saying that couples who choose to marry should make sure they do not violate the moral codes within their marriage. Paul was also admonishing both singles and married people to behave themselves and to weigh well the reasons why they are choosing marriage.

In my premarital counseling sessions, I always ask a couple, "Can you tell me why you are getting married?" I find that most engaged couples cannot give me a valid answer to that question. In my marriage counseling sessions, I often ask that same question, and I find that many married couples cannot answer the question either. Personally, I believe most couples cannot give a Scriptural answer because they married for very secular, very non-spiritual, very sensual reasons, or because it was "the thing" to do.

The divorce rate is so high, according to Yale researcher Robert Sternberg, not because people make foolish choices, but because they are drawn together for reasons that matter less as time goes on. In other words, the force that brings them together—[like] physical attractiveness—has little to do with what keeps them together. For too long couples have based the start of their relationship on superficialities and then hoped for the best.[3]

MARRIAGE, DIVORCE, & REMARRIAGE

Do any of those reasons make a couple's marrying wrong? No, of course not! Paul is probing yet a little deeper to see if there are any spiritual lessons involved. Since marriage was considered to be evil by the culture in which the Corinthian people lived and since married people have more difficulties during times of crisis, Paul was advising singles to wait to get married. Adding a wife to multiple stress situations like the loss of a job, no job prospects, or possible eviction will only cause greater pressure. The Corinthian church was full of hyper-reactive, unsteady people for whom life was like an emotional roller coaster. In addition to this unsteadiness, they lived in a morally corrupt city—much like a modern-day Las Vegas.

In I Corinthians 7:1, Paul was saying it was acceptable not to marry. Verses 27 and 28 say, "*Art thou bound unto a wife?* [Are you married by contract?] *seek not to be loosed.* [Don't leave.] *Art thou loosed from a wife? seek not a wife.* [28]*But and if thou marry, thou hast not sinned; and if a virgin marry, she hath not sinned. Nevertheless such shall have trouble in the flesh: but I spare you.*"

Paul's whole purpose for writing to the Corinthian people was to calm them; they were leaving their marriages—unable to weather the day-to-day demands of marriage.

As a pastor I frequently hear the statement: "I just can't take it any longer." Married people, stay married! Any problem can be addressed and solved because marriage is built on principles. Telling someone "If I was married to him/her, I would get out as fast as I could," is unscriptural. That advice may be culturally acceptable and may even be family-oriented, but Christians should be wiser than to automatically listen to people who tell them to routinely change their marital status without seeking advice from a qualified person.

Paul is also addressing those who are single and admonishes them not to let anyone pressure them into marriage. In other words, Christians should not allow the pressure of other people to make their decisions. Paul also teaches that marriage helps those who have the problem of burning in their lusts. *"Nevertheless, to avoid fornication, let every man have his own wife...."* (I Corinthians 7:2) For the person who is struggling to stay pure, Paul said to take advantage of the marital relationship and develop a wonderful love life with one's spouse. *"Marriage is honourable in all, and the bed undefiled....*" (Hebrews 13:4) Those married couples who are struggling are not advantageously and properly using the institution of marriage. Married people should not defile themselves within the bonds of marriage. Physical intimacy should not be neglected nor used as a tool of leverage against a spouse.

I Corinthians 7:3–5 continue: *"Let the husband render unto the wife due benevolence: and likewise also the wife unto the husband.* [4]*The wife hath not power* [authority] *of her own body, but the husband* [has the power or authority over her body]: *and likewise also the husband hath not power* [authority] *of his own body, but the wife* [has authority over his body]. [5]*Defraud ye not one the other, except it be with consent for a time...* ." *Defraud* means to refrain from intimacy for too long a period of time. Paul reminds the Corinthian Christians to make sure the only reason they refrained from intimacy was for a very important spiritual reason.

God's viewpoint comes forth vigorously in I Corinthians 7:3–5 where the husband and the wife are told they actually defraud one another when they refuse to give physical pleasure and satisfaction to their mate. The only activity that is to break regular sexual relations is prayer and fasting for some specific cause, and this is to be only by mutual consent for a very limited time.[4]

Obviously according to God's Word, affection and intimacy should be a regular part of a couple's marital life. "God is pro-sex; it was His idea. God not only created the pleasurable drives within us but also the proper context for their complete expression and fulfillment."[5] Statistics prove that a lack of intimacy is one of the top five reasons why couples often seek divorce.

Paul taught that being single allowed greater works to be done for the Lord as long as one had the gift of *continency*—"the ability to control one's natural appetites." *"For I would that all men were even as I myself. But every man hath his proper gift of God, one after this manner, and another after that. [8]I say therefore to the unmarried* [single or divorced] *and widows, It is good for them if they abide even as I. [9]But if they cannot contain* [control themselves], *let them marry: for it is better to marry than to burn."* (I Corinthians 7:7–9) Paul is teaching in these three verses that a single person should investigate whether or not he has the gift of continency—the ability to control himself and not be bothered by his singleness. Many people I know acknowledge the fact they do not have that control, nor do they want that control. In those cases, they should get married, but they should not marry for that reason alone. I cannot stress how very important it is to understand that fact; wrong reasons for marrying lead to many divorces.

If a couple will tell me the real reason why they originally got married, I can tell them why they fled their marriage. Those who choose marriage for sensual, lustful reasons will leave marriage for more sensual, lustful reasons. Those who were pressured to marry will leave marriage because of additional pressure. Those who marry for spiritual reasons will stay married for spiritual reasons.

In I Corinthians 7, Paul is frankly addressing the whys of being married or being single. Paul realized he personally could do much for the cause of Christ as a single man. The Scripture records that Paul did much for God as a single man because God did give him the gift of being satisfied as a single man who did not become preoccupied with lustful desires.

Some people truly do not care to be married, and that tells me that married couples should not be pressuring single individuals to marry. The context is that it is just as wrong to pressure a single person to marry as it is to pressure a married person to divorce. I am sorry to say that I find both extremes among Christians, and both are unscriptural. That view is generally accompanied by people who believe that an act of infidelity is reason for divorce.

I find that many people believe an "exception clause" exists in the case of fornication. Committing fornication was not permission to divorce! Neither the book of Matthew nor the book of Luke contain this "exception clause." God was saying that if a spouse committed multiple acts of infidelity which often led to a divorce, the unoffending spouse would not be held accountable for the adultery that had been committed or will be committed if that spouse remarries. Nor will the unoffending spouse be held accountable for the adultery committed when marrying someone else, nor will that new spouse be held accountable for the adultery committed in marrying each other because all, in essence, are committing adultery. Rather, God will hold the infidel spouse accountable for the adultery committed by all three people. That is the real meaning of the so-called exception clause. It has absolutely nothing to do with the right to seek a divorce; rather, it has everything to do with who is guilty of the adultery that happens when people divorce and remarry.

What does "guilty of adultery" mean? Proverbs 6:32 and 33 gives the following definition: *"But whoso committeth adultery with a woman lacketh understanding: he that doeth it destroyeth his own soul. [33]A wound and dishonour shall he get; and his reproach shall not be wiped away."* There is a perpetual hurt that never goes away when two people are intimate outsides the boundaries of marriage. Somebody always gets hurt.

I am not saying that God is angry at divorced people. My goal is to share what the Bible says. My desire is for those who are not married to please marry for the right reason and then to stay married. To those who are already married—stay married—even if you married for the wrong reasons.

I Corinthians 7:10, 11 states, *"And unto the married*

PAUL ON MARRIAGE & REMARRIAGE

I command, yet not I, but the Lord, Let not the wife depart from her husband: [11] *But and if she depart, let her remain unmarried, or be reconciled to her husband: and let not the husband put away* [divorce] *his wife."* These verses teach that couples who are married are to stay married. If one spouse leaves, the other is to stay single. If a divorced person wants to marry again, he should seek to reconcile to his first spouse. Paul taught that married couples should not divorce, period. "As long as a couple is married, they continue to display—however imperfectly— the ongoing commitment between Christ and His church. Thus, simply "sticking it out" becomes vitally important."[6]

Those who have divorced friends should not pressure them to remarry. Let God have the opportunity to work in their hearts! Miracles, divine intervention, and life-changing turnarounds still do happen! I have performed the marriage ceremonies of some divorced people who said

The Apostle Paul teaches "Married? Stay married.

Divorced? Seek reconciliation.

No reconciliation? Stay single.

Unbelieving spouse? Stay together."

that **nothing** could bring a reconciliation. What happened? God worked in their lives and changed their hearts. After all, Jesus said that a couple divorces only because of hard hearts.

Paul says that if a believer is married to an unbeliever, the believer should stay married to the unsaved person. *"But to the rest speak I, not the Lord: If any brother hath a wife that believeth not* [she is not a Christian], *and she be pleased to dwell with him* [stay married to him], *let him not put her away* [don't divorce her]. [13]*And the woman which hath an husband that believeth not* [she has an unsaved husband], *and if he be pleased to dwell with her* [if he is willing to stay with her], *let her not leave him* [don't leave him because he is unsaved].* (I Corinthians 7:12, 13) If a couple is unequally yoked together, they are to stay married because of the two reasons listed in verse 14: *"For the unbelieving husband is sanctified* [set apart] *by the wife, and the unbelieving wife is sanctified by the husband: else were your children unclean; but now are they holy."*

A saved spouse is the best chance that an unsaved person has of being saved. Saved spouses should use their abilities as soul winners to love their spouse into

Heaven. A saved spouse should use the power of a married love to influence his/her spouse to want to go to Heaven with him/her.

The children have a better chance of turning out right. Nothing will hurt children more than a divorce. "Even if a parent is happier as a result of divorce, there is no 'trickle down effect.' Children still struggle emotionally regardless of how the parent feels."[7] Any author—Christian, non-Christian, or anti-Christian—who has done his homework and researched will attest that the number-one, most damaging act unilaterally and universally performed in America on a daily basis is divorce.

For adults, divorce brings a world to an end; for young children, whose lives are focused in the family, it seems to bring the world to an end. For a young child, psychologically, divorce is the equivalent of lifting a hundred-pound weight over the head. Processing all the radical and unprecedented changes— loss of a parent, loss of a home, of friends— stretches immature cognitive and emotional abilities to the absolute limit and sometimes beyond that limit.

Children are dependent on and attached to parents, even not very competent parents. When their parents seem unreliable and untrustworthy, the very bedrock of children's well-being is shattered. How can you rely on parents who quarrel, leave, become preoccupied, or don't seem to care about the pain they are inflicting on you?[8]

Some parents seek a divorce and completely disregard their children in the matter. Nothing shreds the fabric of society more than divorce. "Divorce destroys the reassuring rhythms and structures of family life, especially those that give a child's life order and predictability."[9] However, if the unbelieving spouse can no longer stand being married to a Christian, Paul says not to fight the person seeking divorce; be decent and let the person go.

• **God is a God of peace and reconciliation.** *"But if the unbelieving depart, let him depart. A brother or a sister is not under bondage in such cases: but God hath* *called us to peace."* (I Corinthians 7:15) The breaking up of a marriage citing irreconcilable differences does not mean two people must automatically hate each other, start a child custody battle, and go to war. "There are no irreconcilable differences, only people who refuse to reconcile."[10] Some couples eventually have reconciled in spite of their differences and have remarried because they did not "kill" each other while going through their divorce.

• **God is a practical God.** I Corinthians 7:6 says, *"But I speak this by permission, and not of commandment."* God instructed Paul to write what he thought about the matter. Please don't misunderstand that statement because I believe every word is inspired by God! Paul is saying there is no commandment in the Bible that teaches what Paul is penning. *"And unto the married I command, yet not I, but the Lord* [the Lord is commanding], *Let not the wife depart from her husband."* (I Corinthians 7:10) This verse is a Bible command from God. Verse 12 says, *"But to the rest speak I, not the Lord...."* Paul has some thoughts to share, and the Spirit of God uses Paul to write some of these thoughts.

Verse 40 continues, *"But she is happier if she so*

abide, after my judgment: and I think also that I have the Spirit of God [the mind of Christ]." Our practical God uses the most brilliant Christian of his day to record some common-sense, Scriptural advice about marriage, divorce, and remarriage.

• **God teaches that marriage is preferable from the beginning.** Genesis 2:18 says, *"And the LORD God said, It is not good that the man should be alone; I will make him an help meet for him."* I Corinthians 7:2 says, *"Nevertheless, to avoid fornication, let every man have his own wife, and let every woman have her own husband."* Hebrews 13:4 says, *"Marriage is honourable in all, and the bed undefiled...."* All of these verses teach that marriage is preferable, and marriage has been preferable from the beginning.

Obviously God also knows that staying married requires much effort. I Corinthians 7:33 and 34 says, *"But he that is married careth for the things that are of the world, how he may please his wife.* [34]*There is difference also between a wife and a virgin. The unmarried woman careth for the things of the Lord, that she may be holy both in body and in spirit: but she that is married careth for the things of the world, how she may please her hus-*

band." Paul saw the monetary outgo required in operating a home as funds that could instead be greatly used for the work of God. Any married man can testify about the number of health care and beauty products his wife needs! Paul was not addressing these kinds of disbursements because he was a single man. Rather, many Biblicists believe that Paul was probably once married because he had been an upstanding member of the Sanhedrin, and only married men were members of the Sanhedrin. Because Paul is speaking as a single man to the Corinthians, no doubt something happened to his marriage. He is looking back on that time in his life. Paul definitely understood the cost of being married, as well as he understood the merits of being single and being used by God in a greater way.

- **God knows some marriages will not make it and asks that self-restraint and peace be exercised.** *"But if the unbelieving depart, let him depart. A brother or a sister is not under bondage in such cases: but God hath called us to peace."* (I Corinthians 7:15)

- **God always prefers reconciliation to divorce.** I Corinthians 7:11 teaches that if divorce is chosen, then the person should remain single or work toward reconciliation. "Reconciliation demands a choice. It is a choice against divorce. It is a choice to reaffirm your marital vows and actively seek to discover the intimacy and fulfillment God had in mind when He instituted marriage."[11]

• **God prefers that we make our choices and then stay with our choices.** It is good to get married; but Paul is teaching that once a couple marries, the husband and wife should never change their minds. A person never has to make the choice to be married. Nothing in the Bible says that a person has to marry. The decision to marry is one to be carefully considered. Every parent must help his child understand that the decision to marry is too important to be carelessly made. Those who "jump" into marriage often tend to "jump" out. A couple should step into marriage wisely and with great purpose.

• **God provides greater blessings for those who maintain their choices than for those who feel they must buckle under pressure.** I Corinthians 7:1 teaches that fornication is not the way to flee from sinful lust. Neither will marriage fix the problem of sinful lust; rather, that issue must be under control before marriage because it is a spiritual problem. Marriage is not the answer to singleness or family pressures. God wants a couple who is contemplating marriage to take their time, think through the matter carefully, and stay with their decision.

Marriage is bound together by the care, need, companionship, and values of two people, which can overcome hurt, immaturity, and selfishness to form something better than what each person alone can produce. Love is at the heart of marriage, and it is at the heart of God Himself (I John 4:16).[12]

"And we have known and believed the love that God hath to us. God is love; and he that dwelleth in love dwelleth in God, and God in him." (I John 4:16)

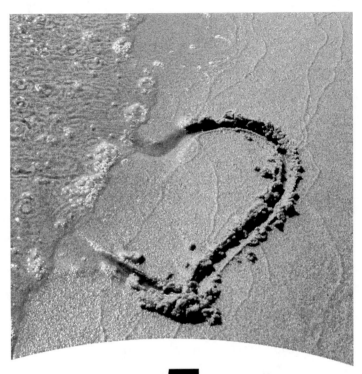

5

An Overview of
MARRIAGE,
DIVORCE, & REMARRIAGE

Man was the only creature God
created alone in the Garden; all the other
animals were made male and female and had mates.
However, human beings were created in the image
of God (Genesis 1:26) and given an eternal soul
(Genesis 2:7), and a mere mate was not sufficient
for man's emotional and spiritual needs.
Thus God planned for a man and a woman to be
more than mates—to be *help mates*. Herein lies
the secret of a happy marriage.

– LaHaye

This chapter contains somewhat of an overview and a review of the previous chapters. The following statements will build on what has been addressed in chapters one through four.

- **God's opinion of single man is not good.** Genesis 2:18, *"And the Lord God said, It is not good that the man should be alone; I will make him an help meet for him."* The words *not good* do not mean "bad" in the Scripture. God was not saying that man's being alone is sinful or wicked or evil or vile or wrong or bad; God simply said that singleness is not good. The "not good" part about man's being alone is that he is alone.

> In the Biblical account of Creation, God's expressed desire is that the two 'will become one flesh.' At the heart of marriage, therefore, is the idea of unity. It is the opposite of *aloneness*. God did not intend for men and women to live *alone*.[1]

What does *alone* mean? Quite simply, man has no partner or helper. He has nobody like himself to help him or assist him. He has nobody in whom to confide, nobody to whom he can pour out his heart, nobody to exalt in, nobody to glory in; he needs somebody to glory in him. God said it is not good for man to be alone.

• **God created woman and marriage to cure the problem of aloneness.** Did God create a woman to compete with a man, to play basketball better and harder, to shoot baskets over his head, to out-dunk and out-jump him, and to out-work him? No, not at all! He created a woman expressly for the purpose of curing the loneliness and aloneness in a man. "God's answer to Adam's aloneness was the creation of Eve and the institution of marriage."[2]

• **God intended one man and one woman for life.** In Matthew 5 and Matthew 19, Jesus explained exactly what God intended. In *The Mystery of Marriage,* author Mike Mason asserts: "In all times and cultures, God's plan for marriage was that it should be a monogamous union based on love."[3]

• **God created the woman for the man.** According to I Corinthians 11:9, God did not create the man for the woman. *"Neither was the man created for the* *woman; but the woman for the man."* It is very important to understand that God did not create women for Adam; He created the woman for Adam. God brought that woman to the man (Adam), and the man realized that woman was who God had for him.

God created the woman for the man for two simple reasons:

Woman was created to be a helper. Genesis 2:18, *"And the L*ORD *God said, It is not good that the man should be alone; I will make him a help meet for him."* The words *help mee*t mean "a help or a helper who is meet." The word *meet* is the modern-day word "suitable" or "fitting" or "appropriate" or "made to order." Using the words *help meet* would be comparable to saying, "I have placed a custom order. I did not buy one off the shelf. I had one custom made for me." For man, God has a helper who is custom-made, divinely suitable, and appropriate for him.

Woman was created to be a companion. Malachi 2:14, *"…against whom thou hast dealt treacherously: yet is she thy companion, and the wife of thy covenant."* That wonderful word *companion* is a term that indicates an intimate relationship that is stronger than friendship.

• **God placed the man as the head of the wife to love her as Christ loved the church.** Ephesians 5:23, 25, *"For the husband is the head of the wife, even as Christ is the head of the church: and he is the saviour of the body. ²⁵Husbands, love your wives, even as Christ also loved the church, and gave himself for it."*

• **God placed the woman to fulfill the man and to reverence her husband.** The usage of the word *fulfill* is "to fill up full." When Dr. Jack Hyles taught about woman being a man's completer, he emphasized the point that a man is somewhat incomplete without a woman in the sense that the Law was incomplete without Christ. Jesus said in Matthew 5:17, *"Think not that I am come to destroy the law, or the prophets: I am not come to destroy, but to fulfil."* Jesus did not modify or change the Law; the Law was perfect before Jesus came. Jesus came to further explain, further identify, and further interpret the Law. What the Bible is teaching is that the woman fulfills the man; she provides motivation. She provides a distraction from sin to keep the man from that which would limit his greater usefulness to God.

AN OVERVIEW…

A wife is to glorify her husband. By glorifying her husband, a wife helps him to know how to glorify God. Most men have no idea how to glorify a Being they have never seen until they see a wife glorify her husband whom she has seen. When a woman properly plays her God-given role, her husband better fulfills his role properly. Because the man was made for God, it is very important how the woman plays her role of helping her husband better fulfill or perform his role of glorifying God. For this reason God placed the man as the head of the wife to love her as Christ loved the church.

God made the woman to fulfill the man and reverence [respect] her husband as Christ is respected by the church. Ephesians 5:33, *"Nevertheless let every one of you in particular so love his wife even as himself; and the wife see that she reverence her husband."* The word *reverence* in this verse is the word "respect." Literally, a wife should revere or respect her husband.

In marriage, a wife is "hired" by God to demonstrate and to show her husband what respect is. God's desire is for a wife to show her respect to Him by demonstrating respect to her husband. Many a wife struggles with a husband who, through certain negative habits and actions, tempts her to want to disrespect him.

The Bible calls wives to respect their husbands (Ephesians 5:33). It doesn't say wives should respect perfect husbands or even godly husbands. It says that husbands—no qualifier—should be respected. Your husband, because he is a husband, deserves respect. You may disagree with his judgment; you may object to the way he handles things—but according to the Bible, his position alone calls you to give him proper respect.[4]

However, God is not asking a wife to respect her husband for what he is; God wants a wife to respect her husband for what He intends that husband to be. God intends for every husband to be the Christ in the home, and God's desire is for every wife to respect her husband as though he were Christ in the home. God takes a wife's showing her husband that due respect as showing respect to Him.

God has "hired" the husband and put him in the

home to show Him love. God asks the husband to love Him with all of his heart, soul, mind, and strength. God desires an unconditional, unbelievable, indescribable, total-consuming love from every man. Additionally, God tells the husband that the person to whom he will show that kind of love is his wife. As a husband demonstrates that love to his wife, God takes that as loving Him because the husband who does not love the wife he can see will not love the God he cannot see. Likewise, the wife who cannot respect the man that she can see will not respect the God Whom she cannot see.

Ephesians 5:33 teaches about the woman's primary need for love and the man's primary need for respect. The husband must love his wife as he loves himself, and the wife must respect her husband. Paul isn't making suggestions; he is issuing commands from God Himself. In addition, the Greek word Paul uses for *love* in this verse is *agape*, meaning unconditional love. And the wording of the rest of the passage strongly suggests that the husband should receive unconditional respect.[5]

MARRIAGE, DIVORCE, & REMARRIAGE

• **God intended marriage to be for life.** That is one man, one woman—for all of life.

• **Some men choose to remain single.** In Matthew 19:10-12, Jesus explains that some men cannot receive how tough it is to be married. Marriage can be a difficult challenge that requires tremendous responsibility, commitment, character, and self-discipline. The person who marries must possess self-discipline, self-denial, commitment, and a willingness to take on an enormous responsibility—not only for his actions, but also for the actions of his wife and for their family. The man who marries is willing to absorb and handle the failures of his wife and children and, in spite of his own personal weaknesses, is willing to deal with the baggage he has created, the baggage his wife has created, and the baggage of all the sins they will commit together. He will be responsible to accept any and all blame.

I would suggest that the man who is not responsible for his own personal checkbook not marry. Marriage should never be an automatic, universal, kick the switch on, turn on all the lights and get married plan. The proof of that is the 50-percent-plus divorce rate.

AN OVERVIEW...

Truthfully, it would be better for many people not to ever marry than just to think automatically, "I am supposed to get married." God intended that marriage be a cure for aloneness in a man; yet in His earthly ministry, Jesus implied that some men should not get married. Some men choose the single life because they feel that it is more accommodating to their level of character commitment relative to the demands of obedience from the Bible. If marriage hinders a person from obeying God or performing his duties for Christ, then marriage is probably not a good idea for that person.

Man was made to glorify God or reflect God in every area of life. Marriage should help a disciplined man better meet that goal. Marriage provides an opportunity every single day to show what Jesus would do in any particular situation. A right response would show others how Jesus loves or how Jesus gives or how Jesus forgives or how Jesus is patient and longsuffering.

In a society where relationships are discarded with a frightening regularity, Christians can command attention simply by staying married. A Christian needs just one reason to stay with his [or her] spouse: the analogy of Christ and His church."[6]

Married people know that it is very difficult to have a good marriage because the couple must display the character of Christ.

- **God originally never intended divorce to be an option.** Divorce was never a part of the Genesis creation. The concept of divorce was not mentioned until Deuteronomy.

- **Divorce is similar to ripping apart plywood.** Trying to separate the glued layers of wood on a sheet of plywood is well nigh impossible. "Divorcing" that sheet of plywood leaves only shredded pieces of unusable wood. The Webster's dictionary definition of *divorce* is "separation, disunion of things closely united."

Plywood is composed of thin layers of wood glued tightly together. The grains of the individual layers are glued together at right angles to bring more strength to the plywood. Try as any carpenter might, he cannot separate the plywood into once-again usable layers of thin sheeting. The shredding and splintering of the plywood perfectly illustrates the shattering effects of a divorce.

AN OVERVIEW...

Genesis 2:23 and 24 says, *"And Adam said, This is now bone of my bones, and flesh of my flesh: she shall be called Woman, because she was taken out of Man.* [24]*Therefore shall a man leave his father and his mother, and shall cleave...."* As I have already mentioned, the Hebrew word for cleave is *dabaq*, meaning "to stick together or glue together." The husband and the wife should strive to make their marriage like the illustration of plywood—glued together so tightly that it cannot be divided.

In Matthew 19 Jesus was being questioned about divorce; His questioners were asserting that they could divorce for any reason because

Combined strength is important. Not long ago I helped my uncle do some remodeling on our house. A certain process required a strong board. He took two pieces of lumber, neither one of which by itself would have been useful in this place in the construction. Taking some glue and a few nails, he made two boards, which alone could not have held the stress of the load, into a single, fused board strong enough to do the job required. Somehow I see God taking two lives, a man and a woman, neither of whom could have made it alone, to make one solid union. What God brings together, let no man pull apart.[7]

MARRIAGE, DIVORCE, & REMARRIAGE

Deuteronomy 24 allowed divorce for any uncleanness. Matthew 19:4-6 says, *"And he answered and said unto them, Have ye not read, that he which made them at the beginning made them male and female, ⁵And said, For this cause shall a man leave father and mother, and shall cleave* [be glued together] *to his wife: and they twain shall be one flesh? ⁶Wherefore they are no more twain, but one flesh. What therefore God hath joined together, let not man put asunder."* Trying to tear apart the layers of plywood is what "putting asunder" means. I personally hate divorce so much because shattered, splintered lives are what remains—just like a piece of plywood that someone has tried to divide.

The single greatest disease in society is not sodomy. The single greatest problem in America is not the invasion of religions other than Christianity. The greatest problem in America is not any of the social ills that headline our news media today. Rather, I believe the single greatest problem in America is divorce. Why? God "glued" a couple together, and divorce is man's attempt to rip the marriage apart. Contrary to what people claim, divorce is never neat and tidy. "The popular modern notion that partners can separate amicably, and even be 'better friends apart than when they were living together' is a preposterous myth. The very fact that separation takes place presupposes unpleasantness and hostility."[8]

One of the greatest causes of every moral blemish in this country is divorce's leaving behind a splintered soul of the society that God created. Jesus says, *"What therefore God hath joined together, let not man put asunder,"* but man says, "I will rip it apart."

Excuses abound for divorce, and I have heard them all. A common excuse is "My husband (my wife) had an affair! Divorce is allowed for that!" Even when immorality was involved, God did not want divorce considered! Divorce was never allowed for **any** reason. Too many Christians believe any unscriptural nonsense that makes divorce permissible. Divorce is trying to destroy that which God has put together. Just read, memorize, and live by Matthew 19:6, which says, *"Wherefore they are no more twain, but one flesh. What therefore God hath joined together, let not man put asunder."* This verse bears testimony to everything that Moses wrote in Genesis, Leviticus, Numbers, and Deuteronomy. Matthew 19:6 bears testimony to every reference in the Psalms, Isaiah, and Jeremiah—everything in the Scriptures.

- **God permitted divorce for one basic reason—to provoke an offending spouse back to his (or her) spouse.** Jeremiah 3:8–10 is a testimony of Jehovah God's being married to Israel and then divorcing Israel for multiple immoralities and multiple infidelities to provoke the nation to return to Him.

> The marriage bond is given the utmost compliment by comparing the relationship of marriage to the bond between God and Israel. The experience of God and Israel was not an easy one, but it was an enduring one because no momentary unfaithfulness can undo the bond between them (Isaiah 54:6, 7).[9]

The story of God's love is acted out in the entire book of Hosea with Gomer's leaving Hosea for her many lovers. The risk with divorce is driving away the offending spouse and giving more freedom to indulge in an immoral lifestyle. Usually that offending spouse eventually realizes the mistake of his (her) sin. James 1:15 says, *"…and sin, when it is finished, bringeth forth death."* Someone needs to be at the end of the death to say, "I still love you." God brought Israel back and re-married her.

> We learn from Hosea that what the Lord expects of a marriage is not always that it can be happy and successful. What He wants is not success, but primarily that deep inner quality of faithfulness which, in its capacity to rise above all vicissitudes and all appearances of failure, is a reflection of the Lord's faithfulness toward a wayward people. That is how we must love one another, with a vowed love that is not dependent upon happiness nor any of the external hallmarks of success.[10]

The book of Hosea illustrates God's one accept-able plan for divorce and remarriage. Jesus states ir-revocably in Matthew 19:7 and 8 that couples divorce because of hardened hearts and an unwillingness to forgive: *"…Why did Moses then command to give a writing of divorcement, and to put her away? [8]He saith unto them, Moses because of the hardness of your hearts suffered* [allowed] *you to put away your wives: but from the beginning it was not so."*

• God wrote a provision for divorce in Deuteronomy 24 because of the hard hearts of the Jewish people. (Matthew 19:7) People will excuse their behavior by saying the Bible makes provision for divorce. However, Deuteronomy 24 was written because of the hard hearts of people who are unwilling to forgive. Because people were divorcing for seemingly every reason in the world, God took control and made divorce a legal process with legal documents that had to be physically placed in the spouse's hand. The offending wife had to be removed from the house, and then she could become another man's wife. If she remarried, the original couple could never remarry each other again. According to I Corinthians 7:

> If divorce does occur, God prefers the couple remain single or reconcile.
>
> If the couple cannot intimately control themselves, they are allowed to remarry others.

• **Divorce gives permission to commit adultery, which God hates.** God hates the cause of divorce because when a person divorces, he authorizes his ex-spouse and himself to commit adultery. In the case of remarriage, a minimum of four people are giving themselves permission to commit adultery. God hates adultery; it is one of the "big ten." *"Thou shalt not commit adultery."* (Exodus 20:14) Adultery terminates one relationship, and it destroys every other one.

■ God's Original Intent

In Genesis God originally intended for a couple to marry and stay married until death. Marriage till death parted a couple was God's preference.

Some people who want to follow God's preference understand that "for life" could be a long time. These people would not mind trying marriage to see if they could stay married for life; however, they choose to serve God and make their service to Him their commitment. These people choose to remain single. This choice is not the best choice because God said it was not good for a man to be alone. However, the choice to be single is a better choice than to marry and then decide to divorce for whatever reason. It

> *The* battle for marital unity is not over until the death certificate is signed.
> –Gary Chapman

would have been better for this person to stay single than to choose marriage and face the pressure that caused him to buckle and seek a divorce. The one who chooses to be single must be very self-disciplined to occupy himself day and night with serving God.

A man who marries and finds he cannot remain married to the wife he chose would have been better to have remained single than to marry and have faced the tremendous pressure that led to a divorce. If divorce enters the picture, go back to the original intent. If you do divorce, then stay single. The divorced person can serve God full-time with his life, and his relationships can remain somewhat uncomplicated. Divorce never splits obstacles in half; divorce multiplies them exponentially.

Some divorced people cannot remain single and want to remarry. God's preference is for the couple to reconcile and remarry. The couple who chooses to divorce, stay single, or reconcile needs to be careful not to start a pattern of getting in and out of marriage.

For some people, reconciliation is not an option. Perhaps the divorced one has remarried. In that case, stay single. However, because some people have tasted

AN OVERVIEW...

marriage, they realize they must have a spouse. In that case, marry, but be sure to choose someone who is saved and one who will stay in church. It would be well to seek advice and to choose someone who has a similar type of understanding so their expectations do not bring them to divorce again. Second marriages divorce at a ten to twelve percent higher rate than first marriages divorce. This statistic represents a huge increase in the possibility of a second marriage's ending in failure.

Seventy-five percent of those who divorce will marry again. Remarriage is nearly as common as first marriages, yet more than 60 percent of remarriages end in divorce. What's more, second marriages in which there are children in the family are twice as likely to end in divorce as remarriages in which there are no children.[11]

Some people search for happiness and fulfillment in third, fourth, fifth, and sixth marriages. I have even talked to people who have been in as many as 12 marriages. I must ask how many lives must be shattered before a line is drawn? How thankful I am that the wonderful mercy of God is available to these bruised and broken relationships. How thankful I am that He allows us to extend that grace and mercy to His children.

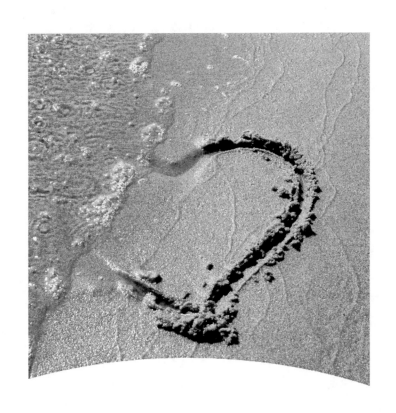

Conclusion

A good marriage is not one
where perfection reigns:
it is a relationship where
a healthy perspective overlooks a multitude
of "unresolvables."

– Dobson

Marriage, divorce, and remarriage illustrate God's grace, kindness, and unconditional love. God is never happy about divorce, but God wants His people to be as happy as He can make them. The best chance a man has to live a very fulfilled life is to marry and stay married to the mother of his children. Their lives together will not be represented by a pile of splintered, shattered fragments from being torn apart by divorce. God's original intent was one man, one woman, for life.

> *Jesus* spoke of high ideals and absolutes—but He loved real people with acceptance and grace.
> –Gary Thomas

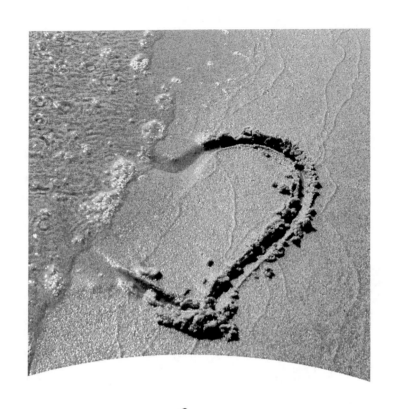

*A Note From
the Author*

Love in marriage is
an unconditional commitment
to an imperfect person.

– Wright

Having a personal relationship with Jesus Christ brings God's grace and kindness to marriage. Such a relationship also brings with it the assurance of an eternal home in Heaven one day. If you would like to know that you are on your way to Heaven, you need to know the following:

- Realize there is none good. Romans 3:10 says, *"As it is written, There is none righteous, no, not one."*

- See yourself as a sinner. Romans 3:23 says, *"For all have sinned, and come short of the glory of God."*

- Recognize where sin came from. Romans 5:12 says, *"Wherefore, as by one man sin entered into the world, and death by sin; and so death passed upon all men, for that all have sinned."*

- Notice God's price on sin. Romans 6:23 says, *"For the wages of sin is death; but the gift of God is eternal life through Jesus Christ our Lord."*

- Realize that Christ died for you. Romans 5:8 says, *"But God commendeth his love toward us, in that, while we were yet sinners, Christ died for us."*

- Take God at His Word. Romans 10:13 says,

"For whosoever shall call upon the name of the Lord shall be saved."

•   Claim God's promise for your salvation. Romans 10:9–11 says, *"That if thou shalt confess with thy mouth the Lord Jesus, and shalt believe in thine heart that God hath raised him from the dead, thou shalt be saved. For with the heart man believeth unto righteousness; and with the mouth confession is made unto salvation. For the scripture saith, Whosoever believeth on him shall not be ashamed."*

Now pray. Confess that you are a sinner. Ask God to save you and receive Christ as your personal Saviour.

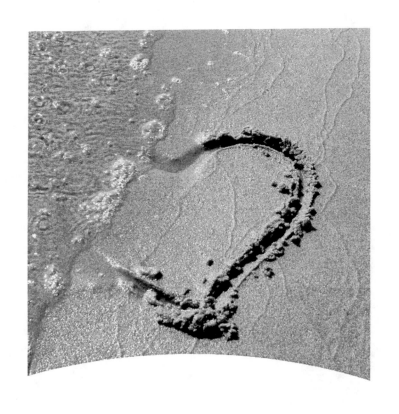

Recommended
Book List

Agape love is the commitment
to build a marriage relationship
whether the skies are blue or gray,
whether in harvest or famine,
whether in peace or war.

– Stewart

Not all of these books were written by Baptists, and some of the authors use different versions of the Bible. I do not agree with everything in these books; however, they contain important principles that can be used to help you have a happy marriage. These books on marriage have been written by very successful people. Either the author has a good marriage, or he has counseled many couples. These books teach many practical suggestions about two people living together and getting along in a Christian environment. Read marriage books to learn about marriage. This list is not comprehensive; it is just a starting point for reading additional information. Disclaimer: this author and this ministry does not ever recommend any version other than the King James Bible.

ANDELIN, Helen B.
  Fascinating Womanhood
ARP, David and Claudia
  The Second Half of Marriage

MARRIAGE, DIVORCE, & REMARRIAGE

BAER, Greg
Real Love in Marriage
BINNEY, Jim
The Ministry of Marriage
CAMPBELL, Ross
How to Really Love Your Child
CHAPMAN, Gary
The Five Love Languages
CHAPMAN, Steve and Annie
Married Lovers, Married Friends
CHAPPELL, Bryan
Each for the Other
CLARKE, David
A Marriage After God's Own Heart
COWLING, Pete and Frieda
Understanding Your Husband &
Understanding Your Wife
CRABB, Larry
The Marriage Builder
DOBSON, James
What Wives Wish Their Husbands Knew About
Women

RECOMMENDED BOOK LIST

EGGERICHS, Emerson
Love and Respect
EVANS, Marlene
Marriage Without Divorce
Relationships Without Regrets
HANDFORD, Elizabeth Rice
Me? Obey Him?
HARLEY, Willard
Lovebusters
His Needs/Her Needs: How to Affair Proof
    Your Marriage
(This book is one of my favorites, but it has one chapter on temporary separation with which I completely disagree.)
HOOKER, Bob and JoBeth
Romance in Marriage—Keeping the Flame Alive
HUTSON, Dr. Curtis
The Woman's Role
HYLES, Beverly
Woman, the Assembler
HYLES, Dr. Jack
Marriage Is a Commitment
Woman, the Completer

MARRIAGE, DIVORCE, & REMARRIAGE

JENKINS, Jon and Debbie
Happy Wife, Happy Life
LAHAYE, Tim
How to Be Happy Though Married
LEHMAN, Kevin
Seven Things He'll Never Tell You
Sheet Music
LUCADO, Max
A Love Worth Giving
ORTBERG, John
Love Beyond Reason
PARROTT, Dr. Les and Dr. Leslie
Time-Starved Marriage
PEARL, Debi
Created to Be His Help Meet
PENNER, Clifford L. and Joyce J.
Getting Your Sex Life Off to a Great Start
PYLE, Dr. Hugh
How to Live Happily Ever After
Keeping the Honey in Honeymoon
The Good Ship Courtship
RICE, Cathy
The Right Romance in Marriage

RECOMMENDED BOOK LIST

RICE, Dr. John R.
Rebellious Wives and Slacker Husbands
The Home—Courtship, Marriage and Children
The Woman Thou Gavest Me

SCHAAP, Cindy
A Meek and Quiet Spirit
A Peaceful Marriage
A Wife's Purpose
Lessons Learned From 30 Years of Marriage
Silk and Purple
The Path to a Woman's Happiness

SCHAAP, Dr. Jack
12 Myths of Marriage
Dating With a Purpose
How to Speak Husband
How to Speak Wife
Marriage—God's Original Intent
Preparing for Marriage
The Art of Getting Along With People

SHEDD, Charlie
Letters to Karen
Letters to Phillip
(Any other books by Charlie Shedd)

MARRIAGE, DIVORCE, & REMARRIAGE

SMALLEY, Gary
If Only He Knew
The Language of Love
SORENSON, David
How to Have a Heavenly Marriage
THOMAS, Gary
Sacred Influence
Sacred Marriage
WILLIAMS, Dr. Tom
Loving My Wife Back to Health
WILSON, P. B.
Liberated Through Submission

The following books should be read three months before marriage or after marriage only:
LAHAYE, Tim and Beverly
The Act of Marriage
PENNER, Clifford L. and Joyce J. Penner
The Gift of Sex: A Guide to Sexual Fulfillment
SHEDD, Charlie
Celebration in the Bedroom
WHEAT, Dr. Ed
Intended for Pleasure

RECOMMENDED BOOK LIST

Please note: Couples should read many books about marriage, especially those that deal with communicating the language of love such as Gary Chapman's *The Five Love Languages: How to Express Heartfelt Commitment to Your Mate.* You can glean practical ideas from any book on the art of communication or communication skill building.

Endnotes

Marriage really is
a relationship of three:
God, a man, and a woman.

– Rosberg

Introduction

[1] Andrew J. Cherlin, *Marriage, Divorce, Remarriage: Social Trends in the United States* (Cambridge: Harvard University Press, 1981) 21.

[2] Dr. Les Parrott and Dr. Leslie Parrott, *Saving Your Second Marriage Before It Starts* (Grand Rapids: Zondervan, 2001) 12.

Chapter One
Marriage, Divorce, and Remarriage

[1] Ed Wheat, M.D. and Gaye Wheat, *Intended for Pleasure* (Grand Rapids: Fleming H. Revell, 1977) 15.

[2] Thomas M. Martin, *The Challenge of Christian Marriage: Marriage in Scripture, History, and Contemporary Life* (New York: Paulist Press, 1990) 21.

[3] Dr. Les Parrott and Dr. Leslie Parrott, *When Bad Things Happen to Good Marriages: How to Stay Together When Life Pulls You Apart* (Grand Rapids: Zondervan Publishing House, 2001) 17-18.

Chapter Two
The Law and Divorce
   [1] Gary Thomas, *Sacred Marriage* (Grand Rapids: Zondervan Publishing House, 2000) 40.

   [2] Thomas M. Martin, *The Challenge of Christian Marriage* (New York: Paulist Press, 1990) 20.

   [3] Martin, 29.

   [4] Martin, 20.

   [5] Gary Chapman, *Hope for the Separated: Wounded Marriages Can Be Healed* (Chicago: Moody Press, 1996) 63.

Chapter Three
Jesus on Marriage, Divorce, and Remarriage
   [1] Dr. Dan B. Allender and Dr. Tremper Longman III, *Bold Love* (Colorado Springs: NavPress, 1992) 104.

   [2] Thomas, *Sacred Marriage,* 41.

   [3] Chapman, *Hope for the Separated,* 15-16.

   [4] Thomas, *Sacred Marriage,* 128.

   [5] Thomas, *Sacred Marriage,* 42.

   [6] Parrott and Parrott, *When Bad Things Happen to Good Marriages,* 142.

ENDNOTES

[7] Mike Mason, *The Mystery of Marriage: As Iron Sharpens Iron* (Portland: Multnomah Press, 1985) 101.

[8] David and Claudia Arp, *The Second Half of Marriage: Facing the Eight Challenges of the Empty Nest Years* (Grand Rapids: Zondervan, 1996) 59.

[9] James E. Kilgore, *Try Marriage Before Divorce* (Waco: Word, Incorporated, 1978) 151.

[10] Dr. Les Parrott and Dr. Leslie Parrott, *Relationships: An Open and Honest Guide to Making Bad Relationships Better and Good Relationships Great* (Grand Rapids: Zondervan Publishing House, 1998) 133.

[11] Dr. Henry Cloud and Dr. John Townsend, *Boundaries in Marriage* (Grand Rapids: Zondervan, 1999) 147.

[12] Lawrence J. Crabb, Jr., *The Marriage Builder* (Grand Rapids: Zondervan Publishing House, 1982) 111.

Chapter Four
Paul on Marriage and Remarriage

[1] Martin, 36.

[2] Allender and Longman, 103.

[3] Parrott and Parrott, *Relationships*, 112.

[4] Wheat and Wheat, 17.

[5] H. Norman Wright, *Holding on to Romance: Keeping Your Marriage Alive and Passionate After the Honeymoon Years Are Over* (Ventura: Regal Books, 1992) 178.

[6] Thomas, *Sacred Marriage*, 31.

[7] Michele Weiner Davis, T*he Divorce Remedy: The Proven 7-Step Program for Saving Your Marriage* (New York: Simon and Schuster, 2001) 21.

[8] E. Mavis Hetherington and John Kelly, *For Better or For Worse* (New York: WW Norton & Co., 2002) 112-13.

[9] Hetherington and Kelly, 46.

[10] Gary Chapman, *The Four Seasons of Marriage* (Wheaton: Tyndale House Publishers, 2005) 136.

[11] Chapman, *Hope for the Separated*, 104-05.

[12] Cloud and Townsend, 9.

Chapter Five
An Overview of Marriage, Divorce, and Remarriage
[1] Chapman, *The Four Seasons of Marriage*, 4.

[2] Chapman, *The Four Seasons of Marriage*, 133.

ENDNOTES

[3] Mason, 78.

[4] Gary Thomas, *Sacred Influence: What a Man Needs From His Wife to Be the Husband She Wants* (Grand Rapids: Zondervan, 2006) 65.

[5] Dr. Emerson Eggerichs, *Love & Respect* (Nashville: Thomas Nelson, Inc., 2004) 18.

[6] Thomas, *Sacred Marriage,* 37.

[7] Kilgore, 84-85.

[8] Mason, 59.

[9] Martin, 28.

[10] Mason, 106.

[11] Parrott and Parrott, *Saving Your Second Marriage Before It Starts,* 14.

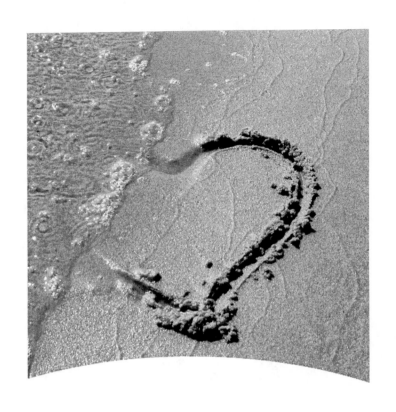

Sources Consulted

To love and be loved by another person
is perhaps the single most satisfying experience
on earth. Marriage provides a configuration,
a form, an institution for two souls
to walk together through life.

– Parrott

Allender, Dr. Dan B. and Dr. Tremper Longman III, *Bold Love*. Colorado Springs: NavPress, 1992.

Arp, David and Claudia Arp. *The Second Half of Marriage: Facing the Eight Challenges of the Empty Nest Years*. Grand Rapids: Zondervan, 1996.

Chapman, Gary. *Hope for the Separated: Wounded Marriages Can Be Healed*. Chicago: Moody Press, 1996.

_____. *The Four Seasons of Marriage*. Wheaton: Tyndale House Publishers, Inc., 2003.

Cherlin, Andrew J. *Marriage, Divorce, Remarriage: Social Trends in the United States*. Cambridge: Harvard University Press, 1981.

Cloud, Dr. Henry, and Dr. John Townsend. *Boundaries in Marriage*. Grand Rapids: Zondervan, 1999.

Crabb, Jr., Lawrence J. *The Marriage Builder*. Grand Rapids: Zondervan Publishing House, 1982.

MARRIAGE, DIVORCE, & REMARRIAGE

Davis, Michele Weiner. *The Divorce Remedy: The Proven 7-Step Program for Saving Your Marriage.* New York: Simon and Schuster, 2001.

Dobson, Dr. James. *Love for a Lifetime.* Portland: Multnomah Press, 1987.

Eggerichs, Dr. Emerson. *Love & Respect.* Nashville: Thomas Nelson, Inc., 2004.

Harley, Jr., Willard F. *Give and Take: The Secret to Marital Compatibility.* Grand Rapids: Fleming H. Revell, 1996.

Hetherington, E. Mavis and John Kelly. *For Better or for Worse.* New York: WW Norton & Co., 2002.

Kilgore, James E. *Try Marriage Before Divorce.* Waco: Word, Incorporated, 1978.

LaHaye, Tim. *How to Be Happy Though Married.* Wheaton: Tyndale House Publishers, Inc., 2002.

Martin, Thomas M. *The Challenge of Christian Marriage: Marriage in Scripture, History, and Contemporary Life.* New York: Paulist Press, 1990.

MARRIAGE, DIVORCE, & REMARRIAGE

Mason, Mike. *The Mystery of Marriage: As Iron Sharpens Iron.* Portland, Multnomah Press, 1985.

Parrott, Dr. Les and Dr. Leslie Parrott. *Relationships: An Open and Honest Guide to Making Bad Relationships Better and Good Relationships Great.* Grand Rapids: Zondervan Publishing House, 1998.

_____. *Saving Your Second Marriage Before It Starts.* Grand Rapids: Zondervan, 2001.

_____. *Trading Places.* Grand Rapids: Zondervan, 2008.

_____. *When Bad Things Happen to Good Marriages: How to Stay Together When Life Pulls You Apart.* Grand Rapids: Zondervan Publishing House, 2001.

Smalley, Gary. *Hidden Keys of a Loving, Lasting Marriage.* Grand Rapids: Zondervan, 1984.

_____. *Secrets to a Lasting Love: Uncovering the Keys to Life-Long Intimacy.* New York: Simon and Schuster, 2000.

Thomas, Gary. *Sacred Influence: What a Man Needs From His Wife to Be the Husband She Wants.* Grand Rapids: Zondervan, 2006.

_____. *Sacred Marriage.* Grand Rapids: Zondervan Publishing House, 2000.

Wheat, M.D., Ed and Gaye Wheat. *Intended for Pleasure.* Grand Rapids: Fleming H. Revell, 1977.

Wright, H. Norman. *Holding on to Romance: Keeping Your Marriage Alive and Passionate After the Honeymoon Years Are Over.* Ventura: Regal Books, 1992.